The Best of all Possible Worlds

recount, and one story often told was always accompanied by an over-serious face which would make anybody doubt its veracity. Whenever I did anything foolish, someone would say sadly, 'Well, you know, when he was three years old he bounced down a flight of stone steps on his head, and cracked two of them.'

The main feature, however, of my mother-made environment was the reliability of it. Some things were right and some wrong, and that was that. Obedience, tidiness, cleanliness (which was of course 'next to Godliness', a phrase which meant nothing whatever to me in those first years), respect for those who were deemed to know better: these were among the basic virtues. Of course, I was often dirty, noisy and occasionally insubordinate, but when I was, I knew it was wrong. Punishment might follow lapses, though sometimes it did not. Major offences might even be put before Dad, a frightening affair, though not often in fact bringing as bad results as one feared it might. About the only thing he got really angry about was if one of us was rude to Mother. And those incidents, I think, came later on.

The reassuring, almost comfortable, thing was that our tiny universe was governed by immutable laws. Something might intervene to protect us if we broke them without malice, but the big thing remained – the laws were there, and they were to be obeyed.

I should add that the discipline under which we lived was not harshly imposed. It was, we were convinced, there for our good. The voice which chided and the hand which checked us were indissolubly mingled with the accents of love, the quick hug, the goodnight kiss, the passing joke.

And then our ordered world was threatened, the house, the garden, the routine, the short run down the hill to school. All were to be left behind. We were to move to a larger house and garden at the far end of Leigham Vale, a move from the known to the scaringly unknown.

'The Vale' was a rather strange road. It ran at right angles to Hitherfield Road at the lower end, down a long, long, gentle slope from right to left. There were houses only on the near side of it, the far side being alongside a railway line, separated from it by iron railings, high yellow brick walls, or a close-boarded fence. The slope meant that at the upper end the railway ran in a cutting, but by the time one arrived at the lower end this had been transformed into a high embankment. Towards the lower end, a branch line of railway swung away across the road, which consequently jinked in a flattened S-bend through a wide brick bridge. The house to which we were to move was, I think, the last but three at the lower end, near Norwood Road, a minor suburban artery and shopping centre, and Tulse Hill railway station.

We were told that it would be a bigger house, a much bigger garden, and more fun generally, and eventually we accepted (after inspection) that this might be so. There was a vast amount of packing up, and the great day arrived. It must have been in the spring of 1913. And then a very personal tragedy descended on to me.

Some time before, my father had succumbed to one of his occasional and usually charming eccentricities, and had bought us a tortoise. He had seen some offered for sale from a barrow on his way home from work. I found it completely fascinating. When I got in from school, I would run through the house into the garden, to see what it was doing. There was something unearthly, almost magical about it. It was only six or seven inches long, but it seemed so self-sufficient, so independent, as if nothing could affect or harm it. The shell was beautifully patterned in brown squares, with touches of yellow and black. The legs and neck were charmingly wrinkled. Narrow black eyes seemed full of an inscrutable alien intelligence. It walked very very slowly with a suggestion of utter unstoppability. When fussed, its head mysteriously disappeared under its shell, and it stayed motionless until, at its leisure, the head poked out again, and it might move on. It found plenty to eat in our leafy garden, but occasionally would deign to nibble briefly if I presented a lettuce leaf to its lips. Water was put out for it, but I never saw it drink.

Strangest of all, it disappeared entirely in the winter. This, I was told, was due to hibernation (whatever that hard word might mean) and he would reappear when the weather was warmer.

All our furniture, carpets, clothes, tools, all our varied possessions were on the removal van, when I suddenly remembered. The tortoise! I rushed through the house to the garden. A search was organised. The obvious places were looked at first, then a more systematic combing of the area, under the delphinium leaves, along every inch of the fences. Ultimately, we could wait no longer. The adults had to help with distributing the furniture at the new house, and I could not stay alone to search on. A barrage of orders, pleas, sympathy, irritation, eventually overcame my resistance. Someone of the family who would take over the house would look after the tortoise, they said. It would be all right, they said. I did not believe them. Dragging behind, someone's hand engulfing mine, I started down the hill.

I wept.

2

Memory

Memory is a strange thing. One cannot set out on such a book as this without reflecting on memory. Why do I remember some things, and not others?

I was reading the other day that distinguished scientists had done much research into the human memory, with very little result. They had not been able to establish even whether it functioned through chemical or electrical means, much less how it functioned, and how its functioning could be influenced from outside.

About the only thing which seems to be established is that the memory exists in (or possibly is controlled from) a particular section of the brain. Presumably, just as aggression can be removed from a person's make-up by cutting away some of the fore part of the brain, the memory could be removed by lopping off the memory part, but the value to anyone of such an operation escapes me. Most of us have some incidents we remember which we would be glad to forget, but to lose them we would presumably have to lose all the things we love to recall as well. All our accumulated knowledge would go, too.

Just imagine the result. This object says it is a woman, and that it is my wife. What is a woman, and what is a wife? Am I meant to stand this way up, or should the knob be at the bottom, and these two extensions at the top? If I move from this position, will I fall over? All the things I have learnt since I opened my mouth for the first 'Wah!' would disappear. Life would be utter chaos.

Memory can be triggered off by any of the human senses. For example, when I first visited Japan in 1962, I kept on seeing out of the corner of my eye a spray of leaves, the twist of a branch, a mountain slope, and caught myself saying mentally, 'Why, that's just like a Japanese picture.' But it is smell that so many people associate with memories. In 1973, my wife and I paid a short visit to Istanbul, where

17

we were taken out to dinner by my firm's lawyer Maître Hatem at a simple but really good restaurant on the shore of the Bosphorus. With typically whole-hearted Turkish hospitality he included in the party two other friends of ours, a Turkish lady and a Swiss lady who was her house guest. The meal was excellent. I particularly remember the chunky salad, every item in it tasting as if it came straight out of the garden. And the last offering before the fragrant Turkish coffee was a dish of wild strawberries. None was larger than half a centimetre across. In colour they shaded from scarlet to white. The aroma was strong and heady, before one ever reached the sharp, brilliant taste.

And in a moment I was transported to a wood in Sussex. It was fifty years before. At my boarding-school we were turned out into the open air every Sunday afternoon, except in the foulest weather, to shift for ourselves. That day I had gone for a walk with another boy. Was it L.R. Goldsmith, a fairly frequent companion? I fancy not. More probably, it was C.J. Timms, known as 'Timmy', who got me into several adventures. Anyway, it was a glorious hot sunny day. We found this wood two or three miles away, entered it over a padlocked gate, and began to explore. Suddenly we emerged into a little glade, filled with sunshine as if to the rim of a bowl. All around was the hush of the woods, the heavy dark green foliage of an English summer. Among the patchy uneven grass, the whole glade was covered with wild strawberries. I knelt down, and the sweet smell rose steadily to my nostrils.

As a matter of record, I must admit that we picked and ate half the thin carpet of treasured fruit in the next hour, swore each other to secrecy, and returned the next Sunday to clear the rest.

The sudden evocation of that sun-drenched scene took only a flash of time. Then I was back in the lamp-lit darkness beside the Bosphorus. Maître Hatem was still completing the sentence he had started when the strawberries did their magic.

Another thing I am sure of, on good evidence, is that memory is far stronger and more exact than we are usually willing to believe. Back in 1956 my wife and I were in Western Australia. We broke our business tour to spend a weekend with my uncle and a shoal of cousins, and they took us out for a picnic in the hills they call the Parongarups. My wife still, on the strength of that day, argues that no chicken tastes as good as one dismembered and eaten with the fingers, cold, sitting on a fallen tree. The billycan boiled on a fire of twigs, and the tea was black and strong, with a gum-tree leaf floating in it for extra flavour.

The simple vista from our picnic site urged me to have a go at a water-colour sketch, 'aided' by the advice of a twelve-year-old cousin and her friend. I touched in the main features with a pencil, and had just begun to put on one or two light washes of colour when the cry went up, 'We've got to be moving.' In case it was any good later, I jotted down a few notes in pencil, 'buff' where the dried grass of the pasture would be, 'brown' and 'black' for tree-trunks darkened by bushfires, 'grey-blue' for the distant line of the Stirling Ranges. Then I took a long look at the scene again, packed everything away, and that was that.

Months later, back in England, I took out the abortive attempt at a sketch, considered it carefully, and decided to work on it. In the end, I produced something which was moderately pleasing, or at least, not offensive. In other words, it was about as much as I hoped to achieve. I had it framed, and hung it in my office, as a reminder of Australia.

A few days later, a grain merchant called to see me about some business dispute. He was a man I had never met before, and neither of us knew anything about the other. As he came into the room, my sketch caught his eye. He stopped in mid-stride, turned to the picture, and inspected it carefully. Then he said, 'That's Australia, isn't it? I can tell by the colours.'

At the time, I had only recently begun attempting water-colour painting, so it was not a question of advanced technique. Moreover, we had only been in Australia for five weeks, so I was not exactly a mental reservoir of Australian scenes. Somehow, however, I had remembered what I saw for several months and across twelve thousand miles, clearly enough to reproduce it with my poor technique, and to have it recognised.

Memory, however, also has its gaps, and they are many and huge. I wish I could remember the author and title of a story which gave me much pleasure. If you happen to know, do please write and tell me. I am not even sure whether it was a short story, novella, or full-length novel. Here are the clues.

It concerned a ship which was torpedoed and sunk during the 1914-18 war. She carried, besides a mixed cargo, several hundred passengers, including service personnel, a large body of nurses, and a group of scientists bound for some combined activity overseas. They were either British or American. The ship settled on the sea bed on an even keel, and so much air was trapped below decks that most of the people survived. In fact, there they lived until some forty years later.

Once they realised that they were alive, trapped, and with no apparent chance of escape or of communication outside, an order of priority for joint action was established. I think it was: (1) discipline and a chain of command, (2) the recycling and ultimately the generation of air to breathe, (3) more permanent arrangements for lighting, (4) removal and usage of waste, and (5) the growth of food to replace exhausted stores. Difficult though this was, it all proved possible with relatively large quantities of fuel and food on board for the transitional period, and a corps of scientists to supplement with their knowledge the skills of the crew, nurses and service personnel.

Later, other issues had to be coped with, including illnesses, death, marriages, births, and the education of children. (Surely, it must have been a full-length novel.)

The most fascinating feature of the story, however, was The Game. It began as a way of passing the time and of maintaining morale, but it developed until it was the basic occupation (if part-time) of the whole population, and the means for maintaining a progressive, interested and competent society. Its aim was to harvest the memories of everyone as completely as possible, and its most common form was for a small group to combine to help one person to recall part of the past.

For example, it might begin, one evening after work and the last meal of the day, with such a question as, 'What happened on your seventh birthday?' The first answer might well be, 'I've no idea.' However, the circle would continue with, 'What was the date?' 'Where were you living then?' 'Who else was in the house?' and so on. Gradually, a full and detailed picture would be reconstructed.

Other sessions of the game would seek to recall and codify all anyone had ever known of scientific and technical subjects, from physics to dressmaking. One nurse, who had sung in the chorus of an amateur operatic society, was able with help from a group to reconstitute all the music, songs and dialogue of the entire range of Gilbert and Sullivan comic operas. And of course all recovered memories were the common property of everyone aboard, if and to the extent that they wanted to have them. I cannot tell you by what means the information was so widely shared. I have forgotten!

After a decade or two of The Game, the community became more of one mind than perhaps any group in history. Their shared body of knowledge, too, was immense. They developed many new technical processes. One was, I think, the provision of fresh air by electrolysis of sea water, which implied a degree of physical adaptation, so that they could breathe a mixture of oxygen and hydrogen.

This caused a complication when they were ultimately found by a salvage team which was looking for something else. The castaways had by then developed the means for short-range communication outside. This was fortunate, for there was an exciting climax with the salvors proposing to open the wreck with explosives, and those they hoped to save realising that this might mean their entire oxygen-hydrogen atmosphere going off in an almighty bang. Naturally, the higher mental qualities and accumulated knowledge of the marooned community convinced the salvors just in time, so that the salvage operations were successfully controlled from inside the wreck.

Is it a fact that every detail of life's experiences is recorded somewhere inside our skulls, and available for recall, given the right stimulus? Some experts and others think this is so. It is an awesome thought.

3

86 Leigham Vale

The house at 86 Leigham Vale was my home from 1913 until I married at the end of 1932. In anyone's life, a great deal happens between the age of six and that of twenty-five. The background, the setting of it, matters too. The street has been renumbered now, and what was 86 is now, I think, 117. But the house did not look much different when I last saw it.

From the front, say from across the road, with one's back towards the fence and the railway embankment, it looked solid, snug and welcoming. It seemed lower, more crouched on the earth than the tall Hitherfield Road house. The front room on the ground floor had a pronounced bow window, but this was not carried higher than the ground floor. The front bedroom's two windows were flush, and there was a low balcony outside them. The house was, I think, built of pale yellow brick, with a few courses in red brick for ornament, and the roof was of large grey slates.

A wooden gate pierced a low brick wall which divided gardens from pavement for all the houses in that stretch of the road, a wall partly faced with cement, and topped with broad, slightly arched slabs of stone or cement. Inside the gate a gravel path curved right to the front door with its two tall panels of patterned glass, and left to the high wooden back gate.

In the triangular areas between the low wall and the path was a dense growth of laurel bushes. For a number of years, Dad kept on saying that they should be cut back, but he was quite good at postponing such jobs, and meanwhile I found their mysterious depths rather attractive. The trunks of the bushes were always black with soot from London's millions of coal fires, contrasting with the glossy green shine of the long leaves which, when crushed, smelt headily of almonds. In the end, Dad tackled the monsters with an assortment of tools, of which a tenon saw proved most deadly. The slaughter was tremendous. The laurels were reduced to subdued-looking groups of stumps. But they recovered, of course.

Round the bay window there was a narrow flower-bed, edged with small rocks. Wallflowers did well there, brave in gold, red and tawny brown, snapdragons (a great attraction to a small boy's fingers), and London Pride with its long red stems, little bright flowers, and scalloped leaves clumped round the base.

Once inside the house, in those first years, I very often would clatter straight along the passage to the back of the house, down the three stairs to the larder, the 'gas cupboard' where the gas meter lived with a garrison of brooms and mops, the kitchen and the scullery, and straight out into the back garden. This was indeed a treasure. Our house was at the middle of one side of a triangle of streets. The ground had been divided up by parallel fences, perpendicular to the streets. Thus, near the corners of the streets, gardens were short and cramped, but where ours reached out to and met the middle gardens of the other two streets, the length was perfectly splendid. You could run there, throw things, bowl a hoop, play a kind of cricket. You could even, as Jimmy and I did, crouch in the cover of bushes in the guise of Red Indians, bright feathers strapped to our foreheads, and loose arrows at each other from our bows, with a horrible yell to claim a hit. Once, that despised younger sister toddled out and wanted a game. Jimmy, carelessly swinging round, simultaneously shouted at her to go away and loosed an arrow. Its brass tip, by sheer chance, cut her face just alongside an eye. I don't know whether the blood or Mother's fury frightened him more.

There were trees in the garden, as well as a long lawn, many flowers, and some vegetables. There was a sturdy lime, with its sticky leaves and fruits, a holly big enough to climb and to supply all our Christmas wreaths for each year's decorations, and at the end of the garden a tree which ultimately became such a giant that it had to be lopped. The biggest bough, eighty feet long, broke its ropes when severed, fell into and almost filled a neighbouring garden, where it had to be cut up and removed piecemeal. We were told it was an American poplar, with shiny rounded leaves like a Lombardy poplar (they shimmered in a breeze) but with wide-spreading branches, unlike the Lombardy's slim trim shape like an elongated candle flame. This tree particularly was a friend and companion to Jimmy and me. It was grand to climb, and seemed to get bigger as we got bigger. We built a platform in the branches (or rather Dad or someone did it for us, I think). This became our secret house. Here Jimmy made his first experiment with smoking. It involved some purloined Bondman pipe tobacco (very strong) and a stubby clay pipe previously used for blowing soap bubbles. The results were dire. I was interested to see that a person could actually go green in the face, and was not encouraged at all to try it myself.

From the garden, the back of the house showed us three storeys. For years I could not understand why so many London houses were built with two storeys in front and three at the back, but when the penny did drop, the reason seemed so very obvious. In the great houses in the West End of the city, the servants were, unless on duty, shut away from 'the family' in the semi-underground rooms of the basement, and slept in a range of attics under the roof. In lesser houses, the same segregation was clung to as far as possible, even in such establishments as ours, with a minimum of support staff. Their areas and the work areas associated with them had to be apart from the family areas, either below, or inconveniently above.

In this house, the working area was three steps down from the front hall and what estate agents called the 'reception rooms'. A flight of stairs facing the front door led up to a landing with a back bedroom, bathroom and lavatory. A reverse flight of six stairs took you up to another two bedrooms, and yet another flight on to the top bedroom. The first two flights up from the hall bore strips of carpet, and the heavy balusters were stained and polished to look like mahogany, with massive newel posts, each topped with a large ball with two incised bands round it. The last flight to what was meant to be a servant's bedroom was plain deal, with linoleum on the treads. Lino, too, was the wear for the whole kitchen area, except where there were stone or concrete floors, which were left bare.

The fact that the arrangements for servants' quarters in an ordinary house now seem strange to us shows how much class attitudes have changed in England since I was a boy. A block of flats I know well in central London shows this even more clearly. It was built about three years before I was born, and was designed for occupation by fairly prosperous families. It was confidently assumed that servants would 'live in' with each family, and each family's quarters were separated from those of the servants by a flight of twelve stairs. They were accommodated not only at the back of the block, but at what was evidently thought a suitably lower level for each floor.

The same general attitude applied to every aspect of life. It was not just a division between masters and servants. There were class divisions at all sorts of levels. I have heard that the most rigid and severe divisions were those between different classes of servants in the back regions of a great house. But in all regions of society there were class distinctions.

Different classes of people spoke different dialects with different accents, though some could assume several different kinds. Mother, for example, enjoyed showing her proficiency in the broad cockney accents she was familiar with in her childhood in Southwark High Street and the New Kent Road. The cameos she gave of that sort of life are still vivid with me. In winter, she said, the hot potato vendor, his wares baking on the pail of red-glowing coke securely perched on the costermonger's barrow, would cry, 'Warm yer 'ands and fill yer belly for an 'aypenny.' She told us, too, of the little girl on an errand to the grocer: 'Two penn'orth o' lard, please, mister, and muvver says will yer cut it wiv a 'ammy knife, 'cos we got company.' And there was the story of the two children, whose dialogue ran:

'Gi' us a bite o' yore apple.'

'Naow.'

'Gi' us the core, then.'

'Ain't gonna be no core.'

'Then let me smell yer breff.'

On the other hand, she could assume with equal ease the prim manners and pursed-up vowels of the trained shop-assistant. Like so many respectable young women at the end of the nineteenth century, she had been apprenticed to a draper's store. In her case, it was in Croydon, Surrey, just outside London. The apprentices lived over the shop, carefully segregated in one dormitory for the girls, and one for the boys. Their hours were long and the work hard. If they were paid at all, it was a pittance, and the employer fed them as cheaply as possible. She was quick to learn, neat and personable, and did well. Eventually she reached the dizzy height of being head glove saleswoman at Jones and Higgins' department store in Peckham Rye, South London. When I was about twelve years old, she took me there to buy handkerchiefs, but partly, I suspect, to show off her status as wife and mother to former colleagues. After choosing my handkerchiefs (white cotton, I think, not linen), we waited while one of the staff with a little machine printed my full name in black copperplate letters in the corner of each. And the whole time we were there senior ladies on the staff were coming up, exclaiming, and exchanging reminiscences. After all, as Mother had told me, gloves were high fashion – the last polish to the appearance of a well turned-out lady. We even had a visit at the handkerchief counter from a middle-aged gentleman of an appearance slightly reminiscent of Mr Pickwick, greeted by Mother with a charming blend of matronly dignity and suppressed giggles. This, she whispered to me as he sailed away again into the store, was no less than 'young Charlie Higgins' himself.

The differences, however, went far beyond accents and vocabulary. They affected manners, modes of address, even bodily attitudes, depending on who was near. All were dictated by one's mental attitude. To those who were in one's own class, one was relaxed and casual. To those in another, one adopted the appropriate pose, gestures and language.

To marry out of one's class was unusual, and social pressures made such a step unlikely to result in a comfortable life. Even social contacts across the invisible dividing lines were rather unusual. And certain areas of society were to a large extent reserved for the more privileged groups in terms of lineage and family connections. This applied not only to the higher public offices, but to some of the professions, and even to opportunities for higher education at the older universities. (London University was an exception, and this was where my brother Jimmy acquired a chemistry degree, financed by a bursary won in a competitive examination.) In later years, a man in one of the most exclusive professions, and himself the third generation of his family to figure in it, told me that in his younger days his severe and even oppressive attitude to his staff was based on a conviction that it was in any case a privilege for them to serve one of his family. The fact that he admitted to that may be enough to show how much he had changed in his attitude later. There is, however, more convincing evidence. He fought for the chance for employees starting at the very bottom to be admitted into partnership, and after some years two of them achieved this. As it happened, neither of the first two proved an unqualified success. The very nice one was rather too old, and never really took any leadership in the firm. The other was brilliant, aggressive, and a source of friction. But the breakthrough in principle was achieved.

I remember, too, another professional man who retained the manners of earlier days well into the present century. I often had to see him on business. We would be sitting, discussing some issue, when he would lean back and bellow a long-drawn-out 'Smi-i-ith!' The door would open. A man would come in with noiseless tread, carrying a shorthand notebook, and seat himself on the edge of a straight-backed chair against the wall. His employer would dictate something, to be inscribed in neat shorthand, give any necessary instructions, and wave him out of the room. I may be exaggerating, but I do not recall Smith being the object of a single glance in the whole process. Even in those days, I found it intensely embarrassing.

There was no complete bar to people passing the barriers of class, either 'upwards' or 'downwards'. Throughout history there have been examples of exceptional people doing this – even some who became Roman emperors. However, in my childhood days, in England, class could never be forgotten. For example, Mother and Father would never have thought of taking their brood for a holiday at an hotel. A boarding-house or something of that kind was more suitable to people of the status we had. Partly, of course, it was a question of expense, but we would not have felt comfortable in such surroundings.

During my lifetime there have been sweeping changes in the class structure in Britain. Some of the causes are readily identifiable. The two world wars caused an enormous mingling of the classes, for men in the armed forces, and for women working in factories and on the land. As an example of this effect, I often think of a young chartered accountant, too young for the second war, but old enough to do two years' national service in the Royal Air Force. There he mixed with young men of all kinds. Some, even, could barely read and write. Yet he found it a most rewarding experience to get to know people vastly different from his rather refined and cultivated chosen companions at school and at work. 'Wouldn't have missed it for worlds,' was his verdict, although he also admitted that some of his experiences in the ranks were actively unpleasant.

Another big change in Britain came with the Education Act of 1944, which produced a multiplication of university places, and made higher education much more generally available. At the same time, social welfare programmes and the heavy taxation needed to finance them have produced a much more egalitarian society. The poor, in general, are not nearly so poor, and the rich, in general, are not nearly so rich in comparison with them. One result of this is the near extinction of the servant class. That may be a slight exaggeration, but in the block of flats I referred to earlier, I doubt if there are a dozen resident servants in 180 flats, which were designed to accommodate several hundred in domestic service to the families there. And most of the dozen are with foreign families, some of them Arabs, living in England for a few years.

There have also been major changes in status in every area of life.

Most British farms are now, I believe, run by the family which owns them, except where a commercial concern treats its farm as akin to a factory, and organises it on the basis of a handful of mechanics and a lot of machinery. Factories were seen in the days when Karl Marx was writing as places were hard-faced men of wealth exploited workers by extracting endless hours of work from them for a minimum wage. This had begun to change even when I was born, and the process had galloped forward since then. Factories now tend to be either small, where everyone is in everyone else's confidence, or big enough to be owned by thousands of small shareholders, and managed by technicians who are often not so very different in status and outlook from the skilled workers. Even in a business like mine, in an office in the centre of London, it was not extraordinary that I progressed from 'office boy' to be one of the principals. Several others have done so since. After I became a partner, I made the rather obvious joke that the change seemed to be merely from working for one boss, to working for everyone. And after twenty years as a partner, I was touched to be presented by the staff with a silver salver inscribed 'from his friends'. I had, too, become accustomed by then to being addressed by my Christian name not only by my partners but by a large proportion of the staff, of both sexes and a wide range of ages.

There have been changes, then, in the class system in this and other countries. There should, of course, be much more. Most of us still trail tatters of our class attitudes, or those of our forebears. In almost all aspects of society one comes against these mostly invisible barriers. Sometimes their existence is denied, but they are there nonetheless.

Some people try to set up against class attitudes a spurious sort of equality. They are against examinations in schools, they say, because it is wrong to discriminate between clever children and those of lesser mental ability. Some say that workers should be paid the same rate regardless of whether they contribute more or less by their work than the man on the next bench or desk. But people are not equal. To pretend otherwise does no service to anyone.

Class divisions are not only based on family or lineage. Cynics in Australia used to say that in Victoria your social status depended on which school you went to; in South Australia, on which church you attended; in New South Wales, on how much money you had. In countries as different as India and the United States, many people use wealth as a measuring rod for class, too.

There is a comic side to class divisions. P.G. Wodehouse based fifty or a hundred novels on that, and by no means exhausted the subject. Shakespeare had a lot of fun with it in several plays, not least in *Henry V*. So did many others, including J.M. Barrie in *The Admirable Crichton*, where in the noble family stranded on a desert island, the earl proved useless, while the butler by his all-round character and competence automatically became chief of the tribe.

The tragic side of the class issue is the way in which it has been used by Marx, Lenin, Trotsky, Mao and their friends to divide the world, and within that division to set not only workers against bosses, but countries against countries, and right down to little groups of extremists against each other. They made class into a destructive ideology which has tortured the world, and could destroy it. I happen to believe that this era of class conflict is ending, but it is still only a hope that this is so.

The real answer to class prejudice and class barriers is to set a true value on every individual. Each needs to be treasured, and each one's gifts developed, used and rewarded. Then we will be in less danger of trying to compare the standing and value of essentially different people. Then we will not have to worry so much whether a cabinet minister is more to be honoured than a pop singer (millions would vote for the pop singer), a nurse than a footballer, a cowman than a stockbroker, an Asian peasant than a top American technologist. And a true valuation of everyone can only be made in the context of an unprejudiced view of the whole of creation. For that, we need to appreciate others as part of a magnificent scheme, rather than trying to compare them with each other.

But let us return to Leigham Vale. Where did we all sleep? This varied a little, according to need. In November 1913 a fourth child was born, a son, though Mother greatly hoped for a second daughter. 'Nurse' came for this, and slept in the back bedroom. Baby Donald was in the front room with our parents, Jimmy and I in the adjoining room in a double bed with brass knobs on the corner posts (the knobs could be screwed off, and small objects hidden in them), and Moo at the top. When Nurse disappeared again, Moo came down one floor, and some kind of servant materialised who took over at the top.

I feel confident this must have been what was described as a 'mother's help'. Surely the species has died out now, but the examples we encountered were very varied. Two of them are still quite vivid to me, in some respects. One was Nellie Vosper, a Cornish girl, plump and laughing, with dimpled elbows and skin like clotted cream. She had brilliantly reddish-gold hair, and perhaps (though I can't have been more than six or seven) I sensed in her my very first impression of sex, for she was wholeheartedly in love with a sailor. She talked of him a lot, and his rare times ashore and their meetings were emotional climaxes of a high order. And of course she went back to Fowey to marry him, and we missed Nellie's rich voice and warm caring.

The other was a great contrast, small, slim and quiet Cissie Hall. I think of her as mousey-haired and wearing grey, the born spinster to look at. But she too was very fond of our family, and I was said to be her favourite. Without one clear picture of any characteristic of hers, or any incident in which she figured, I still think of her as an embodiment of affection and one who surrounded us with warmth, efficiency, and quietness. And where Nellie disappeared totally to far-off Cornwall, Cissie kept in touch with Mother for the rest of her life, after her few years with us. We even met occasionally. For a while, her mother and she kept a seaside boarding-house on the Essex coast at Thorpe Bay. When I was about twelve, Dad took me down for a week's holiday with them. They made a great fuss of us, though it meant even more to me that one of their lodgers was the engineer at the Kursaal, the great amusement part at Southend-on-Sea, and he arranged for me to sample all the spectacular rides free of charge. Many years later, my wife and I drove down to see Cissie in very different circumstances. She and her sister, a notable cook, were running the household of Lord Hodson, a distinguished judge, near Henley-on-Thames, and they got special permission to entertain us to tea in the servants' hall. Dear Cissie. She was grey, and slowing down at last, but she was just the same. And to her this big balding man was still the little boy of long ago.

It must have been in later years that we had a succession of 'live-in' maids, who have left no great impression on me, except that they mostly came from difficult home backgrounds, with sketchy ideas about work in a home. And I could realise that Mother handled them very creatively with a mixture of affection, discipline, and the sharing of her very considerable domestic skills.

I can still see very clearly many details of that house. It was gas-lit, of course. In the two main reception rooms, the hall, and the front bedroom there were what were called 'incandescent' fitments. A small dome made of, I suppose, cotton lace impregnated with some chemical, and known as a gas mantle, topped the end of the pipe. When a new mantle was fitted a match was put to it, and the protective chemical burned off with a blue flame. Then the gas was turned on, and lit, and the mantle gave a brilliant slightly greenish light. It was, however, now quite fragile, and was both protected from draughts and decorated by a tinted glass shade. In rooms of lesser importance, we simply had the naked 'fish-tail' flame of burning gas, a flat vertical gold fan of light with a bright blue tongue in its centre. It hissed quietly, and wavered in a wind.

Heating was by coal fires. In winter there was normally one in the front room downstairs, and always one in the kitchen range. More rarely, for special occasions, a fire would be lit in the drawing-room or, in case of sickness, in a bedroom. And of course there was the copper on washdays. In the scullery, beyond the kitchen, there was a sink in one corner, and facing it the copper, which was simply a big metal tub set into an erection of brick and cement, with room underneath for a small but intense fire of wood and coal. Repeated jugfuls filled the tub with water, and the main wash of the week on Monday mornings was done when the water boiled, with vast aprons, rolled-up sleeves, and a bar of yellow Sunlight Soap. A good deal of muscle was needed, both for the pounding, turning, and squeezing of sheets, towels and clothes for a family of six or seven, and for hanging them out on clothes lines in the garden, and ironing with the solid black irons heated on the kitchen range.

We children spent a good deal of time in the front room, with its 'Turkey' carpet in bright blue and red, its carved mahogany sideboard, massive mahogany chairs upholstered in shiny black horsehair, and the heavy oval dinner table. A year or two later, Dad brought home a boxed set of equipment for table tennis or 'ping pong'. The first bats, I remember, had long handles bound round with tape, and the heads were a circular frame with a taut sheet of parchment on each side – hence, I suppose, the onomatopoeia 'ping pong'. The balls were not unlike modern ones, but smelt strongly of celluloid. When dented, they could sometimes be coaxingly pressed into springing out again into a globular shape.

Our games were a little eccentric, being played on an oval table with fancily bevelled edges. These unusual hazards produced a game with extreme emphasis on agility and retrieving shots which shot off the bevelled edges into quite extraordinary directions. This training may have helped me twenty years later to perform so brilliantly in a casual match against an English international player. I won one point against him in three games, and was vigorously applauded. Considering our respective status in the game, it really must have shaken him.

A less usual haunt was the drawing-room adjoining, with its French windows opening on to the back garden. With its green carpet and furniture of wood stained and polished a shiny black, with green cut moquette upholstery, it both looked and felt a colder room. It was only used for rare evening parties, for the more formal of teas for visitors, and for one other purpose which I can still only think of with a feeling of nervousness and foreboding. That subject was 'practice'. Both Jimmy and I, and eventually all four of us, were subjected to regular piano lessons, and were expected, nay, commanded, to do a certain period of practice each day. This might comprise scales, or picking our way through whatever simple piece might have been chosen for us. I think our first teachers were both teachers at our Hitherfield Road School, who made a small additional income this way after school hours. My strong impression is that Jimmy got a 'good 'un', whilst I was less lucky. Both the lessons and the painful times at the piano in the drawing-room were torture to me.

My teacher lived only a few houses away. When I was labouring at her piano, she sat bolt upright alongside me, and when I hit a wrong note, she rapped my knuckles smartly with a pencil. On bad days, my hands would be completely numb by the time I finished. It was a vast relief when I went away to boarding-school at the age of eleven. I could have had music lessons there, but it was decided that the chance of my learning anything did not justify the expense. So I was free of that burden. I remember clearly the title of the last little descriptive piece I tried to learn. It represented the pinnacle of my achievement. It was called 'The Naughty Pixie Mocking His Mother'.

In justice, however, I should record that on one occasion Miss W. did express approval of my performance, or at least of my having tried unusually hard. As a reward, she graciously invited me to help myself from the rich crop of loganberries at the end of her garden, and even to take some home to my mother. It was a hot summer day. I was wearing a cream-coloured 'tennis' shirt of thin flannel, buttoned down the front and at the cuffs. I thanked her, said goodbye, and set off down the garden. As I sampled the fruit, I suddenly realised I had nothing in which to carry any home. I was far too shy to ask for some container. The pockets of my shorts were already crammed with grubby schoolboy treasures of all kinds. My handkerchief was, even in my judgement, far too dirty for carrying fruit. Yet I stubbornly declined to leave without any. I started dropping them one by one into the breast pocket of my shirt. Doubt battled with my stubbornness, but lost. I arrived home with a full pocket, but looking as if I had been stabbed to the heart. 'Whatever ...', began Mother, but then her quick mind and my halting explanation made all clear. The shirt and the equally stained undervest were whisked off and what remained of the crushed berries were transferred into a cup with the respect due to a gift of love.

Jimmy's musical history was totally different from mine. He played well, and I think he would let me say that he was better than the average child. For a time he played 'hot jazz' in a semi-pro dance band, including his years in college. Later, he went back exclusively to the classics, and still enjoys himself at the piano most days.

The kitchen was the room which attracted me more than drawing-room or dining-room. During the day there was usually something going on there, very often involving the preparation of food. Often I would get called in to make some semi-skilled contribution, like washing currants, picking out any small stones (for such things as smart packets of cleaned and standardised dried fruits were far in the future), and spreading the fruit out on a sheet of newspaper to dry over the stove. A prized job, if Mother was making rock cakes or bread pudding, was to be given a very sharp knife to chop into small pieces a heap of crystallised fruits. These were half-rinds of oranges, lemons, peaches and apricots preserved in sugar, each containing in its curve a residue of the sugar densely impregnated with the different flavours. When the job was finished, I was allowed to eat these slivers and chunks of sugar.

Buttered toast, too, was an afternoon treat for tea. If this had been made in the kitchen, and I had held it up on the wire toasting-fork to the glowing coals of the kitchen range, it somehow tasted far better than if made in the more formal setting of the dining-room, kneeling outside the brass fender, with a matching brass toasting-fork. The kitchen fender was higher, black and businesslike. Alongside it was a thick rag mat, made of countless tongues of black, white and red cotton rags. It was good to kneel on, and if a live coal fell on it there was no danger. It only smoked – and smelt. A few months back, at Dove Cottage in Grasmere, I saw a rug just like it before the coal fire. I think the custodians must have found someone who could reproduce the old craft, but it was nice to picture the poet Wordsworth and his family round a rug just like the one we used to have at home.

4

Childhood games and pastimes

The lessons in Hitherfield Road Junior School seem to have passed through my mind leaving no trace behind. This seems unfair to teachers of whom I remember nothing bad, particularly as I learned enough to sit a very competitive examination for a place at Christ's Hospital, and win one of the handful of places available for the whole of London that year. But the school playground is much more vivid to me. There was, too, a field adjoining it, though how it was utilised for or by the boys I find it hard to say. Probably it was for the more organised attempts at cricket, association football, and athletics, and I was not good enough to be involved in these much. When I mentioned the field the other day to a fellow pupil of that era, the one thing we both thought of was the great row of may trees along one side. For a few hot weeks in summer, they bore masses of white blossom like ground-tethered clouds, and filled the air with their thick sweet scent.

The playground was the scene of intense activity each day, both at the mid-morning break, and the lunch-time interval, for which one usually brought sandwiches and cake. The boys, segregated by railings from the girls and infants, gave over every possible instant to a variety of games, mostly involving a vast amount of running and shouting. Some of them were the seasonal games played by English children for centuries, and revived each year. Examples are marbles, which reappeared when the ground became drier in spring or early summer, and conkers, heralded by the fruit of the horse-chestnut trees ripening and falling in the autumn.

Half the fun of conkers was in the preliminaries. First, there was the finding of the new nuts. We learnt where the trees were to be found in the neighbourhood and (especially after a high wind) searched among the drifts of orange-brown leaves beneath them for the shiny nuts,

34

often still hidden in the fleshy, spiked green outer casing. There is nothing like a horse-chestnut for gloss of surface and richness of colour, sometimes with strange black patterns deep in the dark reddish brown. For a moment, let me flick the picture on in time about twenty-five years, to an occasion when my wife and I deposited our children for a few hours with another family. Tactfully, they had not told me that it was their son's second birthday. Some of his contemporaries had already arrived for a tea-party, and the birthday boy himself, Jim Wigan, came bouncing to the front gate to greet us. We, unknowing, were quite unprepared as regards a gift for him. However, my wife fished into a pocket, and produced a very small conker she had picked up in the road. She presented it to him with due ceremony. His eyes gleamed. 'Oh ...' was all he could say on a long expiring breath. He gazed at it in his palm, then clutched it to his chest with both hands, and rushed indoors to show it to his friends.

The more venturesome boys would climb the trees to shake down nuts, or try to knock them down by spinning heavy sticks up into the branches. The spoils would be taken home. A hole would be bored through each nut with a metal meat skewer, and a length of thick string threaded through and knotted at one end. When conkers were in season, our pockets bulged with nuts, and ends of string appeared at the oddest moments.

In case you, sir or (more likely) madam, have never had the joy of playing conkers, I cannot resist the temptation to explain the game. Its title is believed to be a corruption of 'conquerors'. The defender wraps the free end of his string round his hand so that the nut hangs from the hand, some eight or nine inches below. The attacker, controlling his own string with one hand, and steadying the nut with the other, aims to hit nut with nut. After each swing, the positions are reversed, and the game goes on until one of the nuts is split, and broken from its string. A virgin conker is a 'oner' or – if you like – 'one-er'. If it breaks another 'oner', it becomes a 'twoer'. Should a 'sixer' beat a 'tenner', it becomes a 'sixteener'. and so on. I think I remember a forty-eighter once, a scarred and honoured veteran.

There was some controversy as to whether it was permissible to harden conkers in the oven before battle, but the general opinion was that this was against the ethics of the sport. I am sure that the Marylebone Conker Club (if there is one) would rule against it.

The marbles we used were mostly of baked clay, plain red, blue, green and brown, but some were of glass with a twist of colour imprisoned in the solid globe by some trick of manufacture. Some of those were larger than the common clay ones, and more highly valued when scoring points in games, or when swapping marbles with other *aficionados*. Various games were played, some with chalked areas on the asphalt playground, some against walls. The marbles might be rolled, dropped, or tossed short distances. It was always skill that mattered, not force.

Shortly after we moved to Leigham Vale, I played a short game of marbles after school, before being harried out of the playground by the school caretaker. I was excited by the game or, more likely, fascinated by some small problem of technique, and played a solitary marbles game against myself all the way from school gate to garden gate, which must have been the best part of half a mile. A few inches at a time, it took a long while, and I was scandalously late for tea. I got a tongue-lashing from Mother for it. Its theme was the dirty and ill-bred appearance of playing in the gutter, but I sensed that she had been afraid that I had been delayed by some accident, and this put an edge on her tongue.

Most of our playground games, however, were more robust. I do not know if the two I remember best are played today. One was 'Relieve-o'. Players were divided into two teams, taking care that some of the best runners were in each team. The defending team had to chase and capture the others (by a slap between the shoulders) and bring them back to base, which would be a corner of the playground. Any member of the other team still at liberty would try to release the captives (without himself being caught) by getting near enough to the base to touch hands with them, shouting 'Relieve-o' as he did so. I don't think any scores were kept. The sides just changed places after a while. It was really a way of using up surplus energy, and dodging was as important as sheer speed.

The other favourite was 'Jump, Jimmy Knacker'. Again, two teams. A stout fellow from one of them stood with his back against a wall. Another bent his back and put his head on the chest or stomach of the first, both using their arms to make a firm junction, without undue pressure on number one. A third put his head between the legs of the second and clutched him round the thighs. The rest, in descending order of magnitude, did the same. The result as a long ridge of backs extending out from the wall. The best jumper of the other team then took a running jump from the end of this ridge, to land astride it, as far as he could get towards the wall, and cling on. The others followed as quickly as they could, grabbing at anyone or anyone's clothes to stay on. The aim was to get the whole team astride before any of them fell off, and for them to stay there long enough to yell in unison:

> 'Jump, Jimmy Knacker, one, two, three,
> All over, all over.'

Very satisfying. And if, alternatively, the whole structure collapsed into a tangle of arms and legs, that was almost as entertaining.

I suppose that games like these were one reason why Mother seemed to spend so much time repairing clothes and sewing on buttons.

London boys of my generation had another playground which is not so available to the boys of today. The streets were of course the means of going from place to place but, except for the main roads with their trams and buses, they were all places to play in. My solitary marbles game the length of Leigham Vale was not obstructed by a single parked car. There may have been a bicycle or two at the kerb, a tradesman's van or a milk-cart delivering, but that was about all. Maybe a car or two went past, but at a decent distance from the gutter. A small boy's protruding rump would be respected by a swerve away. Today, of course, parked cars would line most of the road's edge.

The milk cart referred to was one of the more specialised types of the many carts in the streets of London early in the century. It had one horse and two wheels, and the man stood on a broad step at the rear, handling the horse's reins over the centre of a semicircular rail round the three sides of the cart. In the middle of the low cart stood the great milk churn, from which the milkman refilled the oval milk can which he carried to house after house. It was made of some softish-seeming grey metal which clanged when he put it down. Would it be galvanised iron or some kind of alloy? On its side was a brass plate with the name of the dairy – in our case Curtis Bros. and Dumbrill Ltd., of Valley Road, Streatham – and a short-handled ladle was hooked on to it. So were a few smaller replicas of itself, each holding a pint or a quart of milk, and even miniatures holding cream. The milkman would swing off the step of the cart, calling to his horse to stop, and stride up the garden path, his arrival announced with the clash of the can on the step, a bang on the door-knocker, and a cry of 'Milk-o!' Normally, the housewife appeared with a jug, and the quantity required would be ladled into it. If no one was in, a note would have been left on the step, weighted down by a stone. The milk would be ladled into one or two of the little milk cans, and left on the step.

Milkmen always seemed to be cheery souls, much given to whistling, and it was traditional for them to wear a long apron from waist to ankles, with blue and white horizontal stripes. In summer, a straw 'boater' with its narrow stiff brim would top the ensemble. A whistle from its master as he came out from a house would be enough to prompt his horse to start up on its own, pull the cart on to the next house, and stop there.

It was always a great treat to a small boy to be allowed to ride a hundred yards or so in a milk cart, and perhaps to handle the reins, even if the horse never took any notice of the young stranger's signals to him.

Envisaging the individual shape and style of those carts, I cannot help comparing them with those of a different yet strangely similar vehicle, the war chariot of the ancient Britons. A highly imaginative sculptor's version of what was probably a light wickerwork affair can be seen at the end of Westminster Bridge in London, just across the road from the Houses of Parliament. Millions must have seen photographs of the group silhouetted against the tower of Big Ben, with the rearing team of horses, and the defiant, robust figures of Queen Boadicea and her daughters. It seems odd that London should commemorate the savage queen of a primitive tribe (the experts now say we should spell her name 'Boudicca') who rebelled against the Roman occupying troops in first century A.D., and burnt Colchester, St. Albans, and London itself. She cannot have been a very nice lady, and she did London no good at all.

Another kind of cart which visited us regularly was not one in which we were permitted to cadge rides. This was the coal cart, an open cart with a partition down the middle, against both sides of which were stacked the black tarred-canvas sacks of coal. The man or men who toured the streets with such a cart were almost equally black with dust, each head protected by a close-fitting leather cap with a big leather flap falling down over the upper part of the back. Trousers were always tied below the knee with string, and a waistcoat hung unbuttoned over a collarless shirt with sleeves rolled above the elbows. 'Coal-mern!' was the long-drawn-out cry, and someone had to run out and hail him if the cellar needed to be refilled, or for maybe just a hundredweight sackful if funds were low. We greatly admired the deft way in which a full sack was swung off the cart, to land securely between the coalman's shoulder blades. He then scuttled, between a walk and a run, to tip the contents with a roar into the coal-cellar. At 86 Leigham Vale, the so-called cellar was a bare room at the rear of the house on the ground-floor, beyond the scullery. The man had to carry the sacks round the house through the back gate and in at the back door. Many London houses, however, had their coal-cellars under the front garden or even under the pavement in front. A round iron lid, which could be prodded off from the cellar below, covered a chute into which the coalman skilfully shot the coal from the sack on his shoulder. Although raw coal is now banned by law from being burnt in London's fireplaces, thousands of these coal-chute covers can still be seen. There is even a society of enthusiasts who collect and record the different designs of the circular castings. Some of these are quite elaborate and artistic.

As I said, we were not allowed within touching distance of coal carts. We got quite dirty enough without that. But the variety of specialised vehicles we saw about was a regular source of entertainment.

Our play in the streets mostly involved various kinds of movement over a distance. The first thing we arrived at, as we grew out of infancy, was a hoop. Are they still used? I don't know when I last saw one in London. Wooden hoops, nearly half an inch thick, came in all sorts of sizes, from a foot or so diameter for a toddler up to a yard across or more. It was propelled, usually, by taps or harder blows from a round wooden stick with a knob on the end, and a surprising measure of control was possible. To trot or run with a hoop was an interesting exercise, with the changes of direction and speed called for by different road surfaces and gradients, by bouncing up and down kerbs, and so forth. A small step forward from a wooden hoop was to an iron one, a thin bar of black iron bent into a circle and welded so. This was propelled, guided and caught up to stop it by a hook of stout wire set in a wooden handle. It could be banged along with the hook, to roll free in front of you as you ran, or you could keep it lightly in touch with the hook's curve, which made a satisfying hissing whistle in contrast to the hoop's crashing progress over stones and asphalt. My hoop once came adrift at the weld. It was a sad deprivation, but I was escorted to the smithy which still stood then by the junction of Streatham High Road and Mitcham Lane. There must have been other smiths in the district, for the bulk of the traffic, except for trams and buses, was horse-drawn, but this is the one I remember. I suppose that is because it was on a busy main road. No doubt it had been there when the Prince Regent drove his curricle down the hill on the way to Brighton, when Mrs Thrale's coach bore Doctor Johnson past to her house in Mitcham Lane, and for long before that.

The smith blew up his fire, and with a few blows magically rejoined my hoop. He gave it back to me, held out a blackened palm, and said, 'One penny, please.' Or did I imagine that last touch?

From hoops we graduated to scooters. I suppose one can see the skateboard as a more exciting successor to the scooter, but we travelled quite a distance propelling ourselves with thrusts of the free foot on the pavement. I would put our radius of operation at a mile, and possibly more. Jimmy moved on from the simple wooden kind to a much bigger and faster one, painted red, with six-inch black-painted spoked wheels and narrow solid rubber tyres. On a good surface, that could really hum.

There were roller skates, too, not the superb affairs of today, but with steel wheels running on either ball or roller bearings, noisy but efficient. But there was another mode of transport which I think has long disappeared – trolleys. No, they were not model cars or anything like that. They were not pedal-propelled. The first we had was of wood, short and broad, with a very low seat. It was steered by the feet on a swivelling batten connecting the front wheels, and driven along by the hands by two wooden levers at the sides, operating a cranked shaft under the seat, and connecting the larger rear wheels. By working the levers alternately, the backward pulls got the trolley along at a good four miles an hour, so it was hardly dangerous. However, it seemed fast, because you were so close to the ground. The main dangers were down steep hills. There were no brakes, and no release between the levers and the wheels, so if the trolley ran away, tugging the levers out of your hands, two lengths of wood were whanging back and forth at a considerable speed very close to your ears. Overturns also happened sometimes. Naturally, we sought out steep hills as much as we could.

The other trolley, a red one, long and slender, was as superior to the first as the red scooter was to its fellow. It, too, had spoked metal wheels with rubber tyres, and just one long lever, with a cross-piece with a double-handed grip. This swung in a bold broad arc, operating its crank, and it was possible to work up to quite five or six miles an hour.

With our various aids to progress we were constantly out round the neighbourhood, in the little steep roads near Tulse Hill Hotel, or under the railway at the bottom of Leigham Vale and on to the hilly road beyond the railway, or up the hill to Hillside Road and down the four long avenues beyond, running down in parallel to Streatham Hill Station and the main road with its trams. Churches, shops, schools, houses, swam past as our various sorts of wheels sighed across asphalt or went clack, clack, clack over flagstones. There always seemed to be room for us, as I remember it. There were pedestrians and prams to dodge on the pavements, and occasionally a motor or horse van would swing quickly round a corner as we were crossing the road, but they seem to have been spacious days compared with such a press of wheeled traffic as London has now. Winds swept along the streets almost unimpeded, the sun shone brighter, rain was a joke and snow was a joy. Or was it that we felt our freedom so acutely that it just seemed like that?

5

Trams and buses

There were longer excursions than those we made ourselves with the aid of wheels of different kinds, or on our own feet. These were mostly made, with one or both parents, by tram. Occasionally, we would go by bus, or on one of the suburban train services, stopping at every station, and with a constant smell of soot, but the electric tram was our usual type of public conveyance.

The first trams, horse-drawn, appeared in London in the 1870s, but the electric trams did not run until 1901. They were a major factor in London's public transport until 1952, and they are large in my early memories. It was by tram that we usually went to visit various uncles, aunts and cousins, to treasure-houses like Horniman's Museum in Forest Hill, to the extensive grounds of the Crystal Palace at Sydenham, where a switchback railway ended its exciting ride by splashing down into a small lake and there were full-size concrete models of dinosaurs peering out of the bushes in the grounds, to swimming-baths, parks, and all sorts of delights.

Technically, a tram was of course a light street railway, but it always seemed to me more like a ship (not that I ever went on a ship until I was well grown). It is true that uphill and when starting on the level the wheels ground away on the steel rails in a very earthbound manner, but at speed and especially downhill it was very different. Then the great structure of steel, wood and glass seemed to swoop and swing like a full-rigged ship leaping from wave to wave. The accompanying noise could, with a stretch of imagination, be the roaring of a gale. The screaming whistle of the shoe which picked up the electricity and the whine of the motor were a counterpoint to the thunder of wheels on the rails, shot through with the creaking of wooden seats and panelling, and the rattle of the great glass windows on all sides. The driver stood on the platform in front, facing the wind

42

four-square. He drove with levers in each hand, one controlling the speed of the simple electric motor and one the brake. To warn pedestrians or vehicles crossing the lines, his instrument was a loud and high-pitched bell ('clang, clang') worked by thumping his foot on a knob in the floor. His stance at the controls, too, was something like that of the helmsman at the wheel of a square-rigger. On wet days, in the older type of tram, where his platform was not glazed in against the weather, the driver would heighten his resemblance to a seaman at the wheel by wrapping himself in a shiny black oilskin coat.

Outside, the livery of the trams run by the London County Council was dark red and buff. Inside, all was light, for the windows were huge, and at night the small bright yellow electric bulbs were multiplied by reflections. Gliding along in streets not so powerfully lit as today, a tram was a moving palace of light, wheels whistling cheerily over the steel rails, with an occasional sequence of bangs at a joint or the points of an intersection.

Some of the seats, those placed amidships, as it were, were crosswise, each holding two passengers on either side of the gangway. They had straight metal and wood seatbacks, which could be swung over, to let the passengers face either end. When a tram reversed its progress at a terminus, the conductor would march along the gangway, a hand on each side banging the backs of the empty seats across to face in the new direction of travel. The driver, too, would lock the controls, and pass the length of the tram to take over at the other end, where there was a similar platform. From each platform, a spiral staircase gave access to the upper deck – and how our nailed boots clattered as we raced up it. The one at the driver's end was barred by a locked door. We much preferred riding on the upper deck where you could look down into the streets, at foreshortened pedestrians and into shops, and get a view ahead or astern from the long seats of varnished blond pine slats which filled the ends of the upper deck. Amidships, again, there were the reversible seats placed athwart the vehicle, but the end seats were the favourites, where you could kneel on the seat with your nose against the window.

The conductors were usually cheery souls, who enjoyed conversation as they issued the tickets of coarse thick paper in various colours. At their best, these tickets were most informative, being printed with all the regular stops on the scheduled route. Doubtless as a hangover from the days of stage coaches, the stopping places were mostly public houses, 'The White Horse' at Brixton, 'The Horns', Kennington, and south of Croydon 'The Swan and Sugarloaf' and

'The Red Deer'. And of course, the conductor carried a punch into which he slid the ticket, to pull a lever which punched a hole showing the exact place you had paid to travel to, and also rang a little bell. Fascinating! A kindly conductor might let you work it for him.

Mechanically, the trams operated in two ways, picking up their electricity by different methods. In some parts of the routes, there were overhead wires, and a long steel arm from the tram was swung out, and a shoe at the end of it fitted snugly on to the wire. This process was always worth watching, as the connection produced a splutter of noisy blue sparks. When the overhead wires ended (mostly in the broader streets), the tram was halted, the arm was removed from the wire and tied down to the roof, and a steel shoe was lowered under the tram, to engage with a continuous slot in the road between the two rails. Somewhere down in that dark slot was a live rail carrying the current, and along this slid the shoe, occasionally sparking and spluttering.

Fares were cheap. You could travel a fair distance for a penny, or a halfpenny in the case of a child. Local taxes provided a subsidy to keep costs low, and especially for the even cheaper fares for workmen in the early morning. It was for their sakes that the first trams were out of their great echoing sheds by 5.30 in the morning, and not back until 11.30 at night. Between 8 and 9 a.m. and 5 and 6 p.m. were the busiest times, when the main body of people travelled to and from work, with crowds of standing passengers jammed together between the seats. During the day, there was more room, and there were cheap fares of 'twopence all the way', and for sixpence you could ride all day except during the rush hours.

Right across South London there was a great spider's web of tram routes, covering a semicircle with a radius of ten miles or more. In many cases, on the edge of the bowl in which London stands, the routes included quite steep hills, Forest Hill, Anerley Hill up to the Crystal Palace from the south, and so on, but the great machines ground steadily and willingly up them. Only in icy weather did they have trouble, and then each tram carried its own box of sand to sprinkle on the rails to provide grip. And coming down such hills was a splendid experience, as the tram swayed and rattled like a suburban galleon before the trade wind. It felt quite dangerous, especially on the top deck, but the centre of gravity was low, and accidents were rare.

North of the Thames, the network was more limited, but this was made up for by a much more liberal supply of routes for the Underground railways (always 'the Tube' to us), of which we in the south had only the main route south-westwards, and a couple of short spurs, just crossing the river. And trams only connected north and south London at one point. There were certain routes from the south which crossed the Thames by Westminster Bridge, turned east along the Thames Embankment, and recrossed at Blackfriars Bridge, or vice versa. Halfway along the Embankment was the solitary link with the north of the city. Those trams going north swung away, and disappeared into a subway under Kingsway, emerging half a mile or so away in the middle of Southampton Row. I think it was my father who first took me by this route, and I was suitably awed when our great vehicle plunged into the booming semi-darkness. It was quite a relief when it climbed up again into the daylight.

In 1952, I helped to show a large party of Japanese visitors round London. They inclined their heads respectfully at the Houses of Parliament, at St Paul's Cathedral, at Tower Bridge, but there was one sight which threw the whole group into an animated and almost frenzied discussion. It was the workmen digging out the tram rails from the road along the Thames Embankment. Apparently, a great controversy was raging as to whether the same should be done in Tokyo. In London, and in many other cities, the decision had been taken to replace the trams by buses, and in a few cases trolley-buses. It was all based on traffic control. At a few points, the rails ran at the side of the road, but mostly they were in the middle. The double stream of trams was in effect a barrier against other traffic swinging out, and thus severely limited faster vehicles overtaking slower ones, or even passing stationary vehicles, like buses or tradesmen's vans loading or unloading. Moreover, a tram took up and set down its passengers in the middle of the road. Other traffic was held up while they passed between tram and pavement, or else the passengers took the risk of dashing across between moving vehicles. And the vehicles were getting faster and more numerous every year.

A lesser hazard was the rails themselves. The twin indentations (which became three if the live rail was underground at that point) could often cause light vehicles to skid when they crossed them, especially when it was wet. Cyclists were particularly at risk, with their narrow tyres, but I remember seeing a scarlet Morgan car, the low-built sporting two-seater with its three wheels, do a spectacular triple skid crossing wet tramlines, one for each of the wheels.

Whilst definite figures were hard to come by, due to government subsidies for the trams, and for the roads other vehicles enjoyed, it seems that trams were a very cheap form of public transport.

Nevertheless, they virtually disappeared from most cities the world over, in favour of speed and convenience and the fluid flow of traffic. Recently I read that certain cities were bringing back trams, for the economic advantage of moving large numbers of people at low cost. Perhaps they will return to London one day.

I suppose we sometimes used the London buses when I was small, but I associate them much more with later years, after I started going to work in 1924. Sometimes I went most of the way by train – Tulse Hill to London Bridge took only eleven minutes if it was a non-stop train, seventeen or nineteen minutes with intermediate stops – with a penny bus ride over London Bridge into the City. Sometimes I took a bus (route 40B) all the way. But the buses themselves are real enough in memories.

The reference books tell me that the first motor buses appeared in London in 1899. In 1905 a reliable fleet of them was introduced, and in 1907 the characteristic red paint was applied for the 'General' buses of the London General Omnibus Company. By 1911 they were so successful that the last horse-drawn buses were withdrawn.

There have been a long series of models. The earliest I remember had solid rubber tyres and open tops. On the hard seats on top, slatted so that the rain could drain through, or on those almost as hard seats inside, one could tell by feel what sort of road surface was being traversed. The ordinary gravel-sprinkled tar was smooth enough when well and freshly laid, but got uneven and bumpy in wear. Potholes, ridges and such were immediately detectable as the hard chassis transmitted the shocks to the lower end of one's spine. By comparison, the roads where the luxurious wood blocks were laid provided a silky ride. But the worse were those old and busy streets of granite cobbles, where the vibration rattled one's teeth, and when the bus slithered and bumped across tramlines, every passenger knew it.

I seem to recall that it was the 'B' series of buses (each had a number beside the driver's seat, besides the government vehicle licence number fore and aft) which were the first to have pneumatic tyres, narrow and hard under high pressure as was usual with motor vehicles then. Later came 'balloon' tyres which gave a much more comfortable ride, with the 'K' series of buses, I fancy. In the decades since then tyres, suspension, the upholstery of seats, have all changed over and over again to provide greater comfort, and of course speeds have increased a good deal – to the extent which the thickening traffic has permitted, which is not much.

The London General Omnibus Company's (L.G.O.C.) buses were

dominant, but there was a substantial number of other operators. They varied from substantial fleets like that of Thomas Tilling, to 'pirate' operators who might, for all I know, have just the one bus. The battered paint might be green, yellow, blue or brown, and the service times unpredictable, as if these modern buccaneers looked to be in the best area for grabbing passengers hour by hour. Tillings, however, and some others, ran regular services, and wore a livery of red paint, like the L.G.O.C. Tillings even had a logo of their name on the side panels with an extra large T at the beginning, and G at the end, like the General buses' G and L. Broadly speaking, the public liked the 'pirate' buses, and used them freely. Perhaps this was evidence of that streak of wildness, a sort of atavistic anarchy, in the cockney character, which resents all rules, except those one makes oneself. (I write as a part cockney myself. My mother's grandfather was a baker in Stepney.)

In general, bus travel was very Londonish in character, even cockney Londonish. In the rush hours, the buses were crammed, but there was a lot of good humour and chaffing, rather than friction. A *Punch* cartoon of that time showed a bus conductor helping a stout elderly party on board with the words, ' 'Old tight, lady.' She retorted, ' 'Oo are you calling an old tight lady?'

There was no queuing for buses in my young days. This came in during the Second World War, when we seemed to queue for every purpose. There were fixed stops for the buses, where people clustered, but young men and many young women would walk back from the stopping place, and take a flying jump on to the step as (or even before) it began to slow down. Similarly, it was quite common to drop off the bus between stops, running to keep one's balance, if the speed was not too high to make it impossibly dangerous to do so. These things were not discouraged so much by bus conductors and police as they are today, partly because acceleration and braking were both more gradual then.

One morning, on the way to work, I got off the train at London Bridge Station. I was rather late, and hurried down the station approach to look for a bus to take me most of the remaining way to my office in St Mary Axe. A 40B bus had just pulled away from the stop, and was accelerating up the incline to London Bridge itself. It was doubtful if even with a good sprint I could overtake it, but I decided to have a go. At full stretch, I managed to grip the rear handrail with my right hand, made a wild leap for the step by which one boarded – and missed it. My weight pulled my hand down the vertical rail, and I found myself being pulled along, face down, at a considerable speed, the bus still accelerating. I had just enough sense to roll to the right far enough to look back over my left shoulder, only to see another bus following a few feet behind. My grip on the rail became even more white-knuckled. The conductor on my bus was upstairs collecting fares, and unaware of this minor drama, which continued halfway across the long bridge. Then a passenger from inside the bus came out on the platform, grabbed the rail with one hand and me with the other, and hauled me on board. My shoes were worn away at the toe-caps, but apart from that I was none the worse – only hot, dirty, and feeling that I looked a fool.

The L.G.O.C. was bought up by the chief underground railway company, and itself absorbed the Tilling buses and other independents. In theory, at least, the buses and tubes have been run as an integrated system for many of the years since, under public control. There has, however, been little co-operation with the ordinary railway network, which is also vital to London's transport. As I write, various plans for the future are being mooted, including a revival of private bus companies. But surely a co-ordinated plan of some kind is essential. An incredible army of people move in to work in central London daily, and out again, of course. The planners were saying a few years back that the figure for the City of Westminster area alone was 550,000. The full total must be well over a million. Yet it still seems that no one is prepared to insist on a system by which buses, tubes, trains and all the other elements fit together.

6

Father

Looking back across the years, it seems to me that my father must have affected my life and development much more than I have been inclined to think. It is hard to judge. Partly this is because he had a somewhat inscrutable quality, and it was not until late in his life that I began to understand him. Only then could I make some adequate return for the very deep affection which he had for us children, an affection he often concealed with a joke or a change of subject.

It was often difficult to know whether he was serious or joking. Every now and then he would start talking about times past. Some of these stories were so strange to me in the early years that I assumed he was making them up to amuse me and the others. 'My father married twice,' he would say. 'He had four children by the first wife, and eight more by the second.' This was I think, quite true. 'I'm one hundred per cent Irish, because Father and Grandfather both went back to Ireland to find a good Irish girl to marry.' This was (as I established long afterwards) certainly not wholly true, as Dad's parents were both shown as English on the marriage certificate. 'We were landed people in Ireland once.' This we all considered pure fantasy, but later found it to be entirely correct. When I was in Ireland in 1984, the present owner of Ledwithstown House showed us various records, including one of a gift by a Ledwith of that time to relieve those suffering from the potato famine in 1846.

It is true that I never established the descent of my family, generation by generation by generation, from the Ledwiths of Ledwithstown. It might be possible by a lengthy search of parish records in the Irish Republic and in England. However, Dad told us that in his youth a young man from County Longford visited the family in Croydon, Surrey, and actually showed them the title deeds of the house which he said he had taken away after a family quarrel.

49

The youth claimed to be the heir. Dad certainly believed him. Like Jimmy and various other relations, I have paid several visits to Ledwithstown House, which is near Ballymahon, some eight miles from Longford town itself. Surrounded by rich farmland where the present owner fattens cattle, it is near the trout-filled Lough Rea, near the very centre of Ireland. There are Ledwiths all around, though those I met say they are from another branch of the family, which moved down from adjoining West Meath. One had a building business, and is now housing manager for Longford. Another has a shop in the High Street. A third runs a filling station near Ballymahon.

The house, they say, was sold out of the Ledwith family in or about 1904. It was built in 1749, a handsome smallish Georgian style country mansion, of a rather unusual design. In floor plan it is square with a central hallway, and two storeys over a deep semi-basement. When my brother visited it in the twenties, and for years after that, the house was empty except perhaps for a caretaker or a sort of squatter, said to be a poet, I believe. The owner was farming the land, and living in a modern house nearby. On later visits, grass was growing in the front steps, and jackdaws nesting in the roof. Substantial damage, too, was done by a fire. However, in 1984, my wife and I were warmly received there by a grandson of the Feeney who first acquired it, and who was living with his wife and children in the spacious basement, while the house was gradually being restored. They were hopeful of completing this work 'if funds lasted out', and had been promised some practical help of a labouring nature by members of the Georgian Society of Ireland. The roof had been repaired, but there were still gaping holes in the floors and extensive work needed to restore the fire damage. Specialist workers would be needed, perhaps from Dublin, to deal with the delicate plaster mouldings in some rooms.

We were shown some of the architects' drawings of the house and other historic documents. It did much to make me feel part of a tradition spanning the centuries. What sort of people had the Ledwiths been at Ledwithstown? There were a few traces in reference books. When one did come across the family they usually seemed to be land-owning people, 'gentry', as some would say, 'county people'. At times, however, I suspect that they subsided into obscurity and poverty, and then struggled up to property-owning again. The style of the house suggested an Anglo-Irish background, 'the Protestant connection', but with such an old family, nearly eight centuries in Ireland, they must have been wholly Irish and wholly Catholic. My young brother had come across a coat of arms, even, a rather elegant and simple one, which suggested it was of some age. The shield was black, bearing a silver chevron between three 'caps of maintenance' of red velvet, edged with ermine. Heraldically, I think it would be 'Sable, a chevron argent between three châpeaux'. Thinking of these things always brings back a picture of my father, with his watchful eye and quizzical smile.

In fact, I think the stories we regarded as likely to be Dad's inventions about the family may have been embroidered a little to make them more entertaining, but they were almost certainly historical. 'One of my half-brothers got drowned through driving a pony and trap into the River Lea when he was drunk.' Nearly a century later one Terry Ledwith ran a filling station and garage in the Lea Bridge Road in East London. He could have been a descendant. It's an uncommon name in England. 'Of course, the rich man of the family was the one who kept the pawnshop at New Cross Gate.' Some years later, as we went past New Cross Gate in a tram, Dad pointed out where the pawnshop had been. 'A half-brother of mine had a piggery in Bermondsey, where he used to fatten the pigs with waste from the London hotels and restaurants. You'd find halves of chickens and whole loaves of bread in that waste. Twice he took me out into Kent in a horse and cart, buying scrawny-looking pigs from the farmers.'

Dad had a restful quality, too, and could be happily silent for hours with a pipe of tobacco and a newspaper or a book. His gardening style was something of a peaceful potter; he got a lot done, but he took his time. If he went for a walk round the streets, there was sure to be time for a chat or two over a gate or a hedge, maybe with a friend or with a total stranger. I picture myself bouncing a ball, kicking at stones, or just fidgeting around until the chat meandered to a stop, and he raised a couple of fingers towards a hat brim in salute as he turned away. On these expeditions, he swung a polished walking-stick, with a plain gold band below the handle, and wore a trilby hat (usually brown) with a wide-ribbed silk ribbon, the brim pulled well down over his eyes. Or sometimes a bowler.

In general, however, I cannot sort out the mental pictures of Dad over the years at all well. My general impression of him was the same at all ages. Occasionally irascible, he on rare occasions broke out in a wild rage, but it was over very quickly. Once I did something outrageous, and with a roar he chased me up the garden with a spade. I was terrified, and ran like a scalded rabbit. Looking back before dodging behind the great poplar tree, I saw him far behind, turning back towards the house quite slowly, and looking at the spade in his hands with curiosity, as if he had never seen such a thing before.

He loved a joke, and it might be a somewhat vulgar one, like the traditional English seaside postcard. One of his stories was of the man at the football match who was anointed by a bird flying overhead. 'Just my luck,' he complained to his friend, 'Thirty thousand people here, and that bird had to pick on me.' 'You're lucky,' retorted his friend, 'it might have been a cow.' Now I think of it, some people might classify that as an 'Irish' joke – what the Irish call a Kerry joke. Some think such stories picture the Irish as lacking in the normal supply of intelligence. I disagree. My theory is that the Irish have a slightly different system of logic from the English and other less fortunate races, and I invite the reader faced with an 'Irish' joke to apply this in assessing it.

One Christmas, we had a rather larger family gathering than usual, with a wide span of ages. Dad disappeared at one point with our youngest aunt, Mother's youngest sister. He reappeared after a few minutes, looking very innocent. A quarter of an hour later, in comes Auntie Margaret, completely rigged out in Dad's evening dress suit, 'boiled' shirt and all. In those days, this was quite a dashing thing to do. There was of course a lot of noise and laughter over it, but curiously enough it was another aspect of that day which was more remembered. Another guest was Mother's eldest sister, maybe twenty or more years older than Margaret. Her main contribution to the day's proceedings was to sit quietly in a corner with a glass of port and (according to the family legend) murmur at intervals to anyone within range, 'It's nice to be together, dear.' This phrase became a treasured possession, and on any unsuitable occasion, such as a picnic flooded out by a thunderstorm, Dad or someone would be sure to say sentimentally, 'Well, it's nice to be together, dear.' It never failed to restore our spirits.

As regards entertainment, he was brought up on the late Victorian music hall tradition. As soon as we were old enough to stay up late, we grew to expect a Christmas visit to the pantomime. We children of course were fascinated by the transformation scenes and the slapstick humour, but Dad also remarked appreciatively on the obviously feminine charms of the 'principal boy'. Long years later, maybe in the nineteen fifties, my wife and I took my parents to see a programme of ballet. Mother was rather keen to go, but Dad almost had to be tied and carried. He couldn't imagine anyone choosing such an insipid form of entertainment. However, after twenty minues or so, he settled down in his stall, and began to enjoy it. At the interval, he turned to me and said, 'Did you hear that Edgar Wallace gangster play on the radio last night?' 'No,' I said. 'It was jolly good.' Pause. 'You know, this is quite different.' It was a programme which included a group of short divertissements in which the young dancers showed off individual skills. One of the girls was noticeably overweight, by twenty or thirty pounds. I think she reminded Dad of the strapping music hall stars of his youth. He persuaded me to look up her name in the programme. It was Hélène de Ste. Croix, or something like that. 'Ah,' said Dad, 'that Nellie's a fine girl.'

These are perhaps trivialities. Two big characteristics of his made little or no impression on me until much later. One was his thorough competence at his work. The other was his public spiritedness which led him to give years of service to the Lambeth Borough Council and to the City of London Police Reserve. Perhaps they are two aspects of the same quality – reliability. People relied on him, and he always justified that trust.

His police duties can be dealt with in my next chapter. I have written in another book of his Council work. I do not think he enjoyed it much, but he was extremely conscientious about it, and spent hours at home on his papers, especially when he was simultaneously chairman of the housing and the highways committees. I believe he twice refused the mayoralty, mainly because he could not afford it. In those days the mayor himself had to pay most if not all of the heavy personal expenses he had during his year of office. Dad was little interested in party politics, and not at all in personal power or position. He had to give up the Council after nine years, but only because his exacting job and growing family made it impossible to devote the long hours he felt to be essential. However, even in this setting his somewhat quirky and humorous mind sometimes broke out into the open. At one Council meeting, a proposition was put forward that the words: 'LOOK BOTH WAYS' should be inscribed in the roadway at the rather tricky point where the trams came off Westminster Bridge. Such items usually were passed on the nod, but Dad got to his feet and queried it. How could anyone look both ways, he asked, unless he happened to be cross-eyed? There was a storm of laughter, which flabbergasted him, for he was trying to make a serious point. Then he sat down and glanced at the councillor in the next seat, who proved to be the only member of the Council who was cross-eyed.

As for Dad's business life, he was able later to set up on his own, and deal with every angle of running a business with modest but definite success. The best proof of his competence may, however, be in his years with his old firm. He joined them straight from school at the age of fourteen, and stayed with them for some forty years. The firm had a printing and stationery shop near Ludgate Hill, but their main business was as jobbing printers. The machines were on the top floor of an oldish building in Great Saffron Hill, in that curious area of London between Hatton Garden, the centre of the diamond trade, and Smithfield meat market. In Dad's early years there, this was the Italian quarter, and the simple old-fashioned ice-cream, or 'hokey-pokey', was made in a back room of many of the houses.

Dad described himself as a commercial traveller, and officially that was what he was. His job was to market the firm's services. But in practice he was much more than that. Over the years he built up the knowledge and the relationships with his employers and colleagues which made it possible for him to quote firm prices to customers for the jobs they wanted done, and (as he put it) to 'see the job through the works'. This entailed discussing it with the production people, to ensure that the planning, style, type-faces, paper and the whole production were satisfactory to him and pleasing to the customer. In most printing firms prices are set or at least must be approved by the financial experts, the accountants or whatever they may be called. And the technical work is solely the preserve of the production people. The man who got the order interferes in such matters at his peril – which means he doesn't interfere. But Dad had both the expertise and the diplomacy to do it the other way.

Once in later years, when I was in business myself, he told me of how he got certain business from the chairman of a company producing medicines. I forgot how he got to know this rather impressive gentleman, who confided in Dad about the difficulties he was having with his firm's printers. He had set his heart on changing and modernising his firm's image. The products were marketed under his name, and he wanted a facsimile of his signature to be the central motif of all the printing. The people doing the art work at the printing company kept suggesting different styles for the name, a smoother script, and so forth, whereas the customer had set his heart on having his name in his own handwriting. It was evident that the experts considered his writing to be ugly, rather than seemly, and possibly even difficult to read. 'They seem to think my writing's illegible', he complained. Dad asked if he could see the various versions, 'just out of interest', and was invited to the customer's house to inspect them over a drink. His verdict was, 'Well, I think your own signature shows a great deal of character.' So Dad's firm got the printing contract for the notepaper, packaging, leaflets and much else besides. He worked on the details indefatigably, of course.

After Dad had got established in business on his own, my firm met with some difficulties in its printing and stationery requirements. One of my colleagues decided to try whether my father's virtually one-man outfit (it was really an agency) could help. The first test was with the permanent binding of some very large loose-leaf books which were specially designed for us. When bound, they were over two feet broad and weighed nearly ten pounds. This was in wartime, and materials were short. The usual people got slower until they were taking four months to get one book bound. During this period the sheets were not available for reference, which was a great nuisance. Dad, using his enormous knowledge of the trade, found someone who did the work just as well in four weeks. One thing led to another, and it was found that he could get work done properly in any branch of printing and stationery, from specialised ruling of paper with those neat blue and red lines for accounting to block-making for illustrations. Paper, too, of any kind could be found. He once told me that he ran an account with every paper merchant in London.

A generation later, I went straight from school into business. I never quite matched Dad, who seemed to know every single aspect of the printing trade. There were two subjects at least in my insurance office where I was really ignorant. I never learnt any shorthand, and I avoided anything to do with computers. They came in rather late in my business career, and I decided that it would be best to leave computers to the experts. For all I knew, they might bite. But I dabbled in almost everything else. So perhaps a little of Dad's outlook on life did rub off on me.

7

War. 1914 to 1918

Of those who may read this, some may not have experienced a major war. Others will remember the war of 1939 to 1945, World War II, the 'Hitler War'. Some, like myself, will also remember World War I, the war of 1914 to 1918 or, if one wants to be pedantic, 1919, since November 1918 brought only an armistice, and the peace treaty was not signed until the following year.

It seems very odd to me that that first 'Great War', as we used to call it, made so little impression on me as a boy. I was seven years old when it began, but my specific memories of it are like a boxful of blurred snapshots, not a consecutive record.

The first thing which springs to mind is air raids. The warning given in London was itself frightening, the bang of a maroon, not the whooping sirens of the Second World War. I think that the first one I was excited by was a daylight raid, when we all rushed into the garden in the morning sunlight to see shining specks, which were aircraft, and little dark puffs, which were anti-aircraft shells bursting, some five miles away over the centre of London. It was exciting but not frightening.

The same could be said of the one time I saw a Zeppelin. It was at night, and I was snatched out of bed and taken out into the garden, wrapped in a blanket, to see it. The great airship was a tiny, distant golden strip, apparently supported above the horizon by a straddle of searchlight beams meeting on it. Tiny blinks of light around it were shell-bursts. I have it in mind that it was the 'Zepp' brought down at Cuffley in Hertfordshire by a fighter plane. Can that have been so? It must have been twenty-five or thirty miles from Leigham Vale. But perhaps it is just possible on a clear night.

Other memories are more unnerving, of night raids both by Zeppelins and by the growling aeroplanes called Gothas, of the slapping cracks of anti-aircraft guns from the road parallel to ours, beyond the railway, and even once or twice of fragments of shell casing rattling down the slates of our own roof. On these occasions the drill was for us children to be hustled downstairs to the front room and put under that massive mahogany dining table. Dad would dump a mattress on top of it, and we would play with lead soldiers or something on the blue and red carpet below. In a lull, Dad would teach Jimmy and me the rudiments of chess, and on one rather noisy night I actually beat Dad in one game, a feat I am not sure I ever equalled in later life. Of course, my attention was on the game, and his was not.

The actual damage done to London by air raids was limited. There were casualties, and ruined houses, but it was not enough to affect the city generally. Aviation was still in its infancy. I knew a man who flew on the biggest air-raid of the 1914-1918 war. The entire British bombing capacity was concentrated on an attack on Cologne late in 1918. The aggregate weight of the bombs dropped was (he said) about five tons. Twenty-five years later, in the Second World War, there were a number of attacks by over one thousand bombers at a time, each aircraft carrying more than the total dropped on Cologne in 1918.

Food was the second area in which the war affected me. It is a matter of great importance to a small boy. We were not, I think, ever really hungry. Mother made sure that there was always something filling available. There was a shelf in the kitchen where usually several loaves were awaiting consumption. Bowls of porridge, rice puddings and their less appreciated sisters semolina and tapioca, great bread puddings wet and fruity inside and crisp outside, potatoes boiled or baked with or without their skins meant that we never had aching gaps unfilled. However, many items of diet began to disappear or become rare — fruits from overseas, sugar, butter and its new substitute margarine. Later, bread was adulterated, and even potatoes were hard to get.

I found my playtime reduced more and more by the struggle to get food. There was no rationing until the war was nearly over, I believe, so any of the family who was available had to go and queue at the grocer's, the butcher's or the greengrocer's. Sometimes, one would stand in line for an hour or two hours, and come away with two ounces of margarine, or shuffle up to a vegetable stall only to hear 'No more potatoes'.

To provide a fresh source of protein, Dad somehow got hold of a few pullets, and knocked together a somewhat rickety hen-house in the back garden. I learnt a certain amount about these strange fowl. 'Rhode Island Reds' was their odd description. They ate raw grain, and any food scraps which might not be eaten by us. Strangely, too, they ate little chips of flint, to help them digest the other stuff. They were pretty undiscriminating. Once Dad brought home a bag of foul-smelling stuff, which he said was damaged maize from a torpedoed ship. They ate it enthusiastically. I formed a low opinion of their intelligence.

But Mother was delighted to have a source of eggs, which were hard to come by in the shops. Those the hens produced rolled out of the nesting boxes into a narrow trough on the side of the hen-house. They were lovingly collected, marked in pencil with the number of pence they would have cost in the shops (usually five, six or seven pence each, but it went up to tenpence at one point), and kept until used in a cracked vegetable dish set aside for the purpose on the kitchen dresser.

It may be assumed from these procedures that money was tight. I think it must have been, though this was not the kind of subject my parents discussed in front of the children. I do know that in those years Jimmy and I hit on a scheme which for a time supplemented our meagre pocket money in a very satisfactory manner. We had been bitten by the stamp-collecting craze, and each had enough of a collection to be quite interesting. We also began to accumulate a stock of duplicates. Sometimes one of these could be exchanged for a stamp we wanted from another boy at school. Then we developed a better idea. Why not copy the shops which sold envelopes containing, say, '10 stamps of the British Empire for 2d.'? We started cutting out paper to make envelopes, filling them with a mixture of stamps, and putting a description and price on the outside, with one of the better ones stuck on with a 'stamp hinge' to attract the buyers. Soon we were doing quite a trade, and working hard to package a continuing supply. We even bought a few big packets of mixed stamps, to keep up our stocks.

Alas, the bonanza was short-lived, and for the most capitalist of reasons. We got greedy; we included worthless British stamps in our selections, and generally reduced the quality of the packets, to increase our profits. This was resented. The word went round that those Ledwith kids were a stingy lot. Our market disappeared even more suddenly than it had evolved.

I wonder if this incident was the first experience to feed one of my violent opinions, and one which I still hold, that if anyone sets out merely to make money, he will probably fail to do so. On the other hand, if someone sets out to provide goods or services which are really needed, he is likely to do well from it. In fact, I hold that most of the time nowadays we are trying to run industry and commerce with our thinking upside down. If we are just out for profits or for a job, or even jobs for my crowd, we may be on a self-defeating programme. We need to think out what needs to be done, and set about doing it. Then it's at least probable that people will be prepared to pay us for doing it.

There were numerous other detailed ways in which the war affected us. Jimmy started in 1916 or so at a secondary school (the Strand School off Brixton Hill) and found among his fellow pupils a group of Serbian boys who had arrived as refugees. He learnt the Cyrillic alphabet from one of them, which helped us in identifying stamps from East European countries. Our schools stopped giving the usual books as prizes for good work. All we got was a measly certificate. I still have one or two of them, but I was not much of a one for winning prizes.

Dad was thirty-seven years old when the war broke out, so there was no question of his joining the fighting services. His eyes were bad, too. He volunteered for the City of London Police Reserve, was gladly accepted, and did a good load of evening and night duty relieving the regular police. His accounts of this were, I think, strongly twisted towards entertaining us, and censoring out the tiring and occasionally dangerous elements. When there were air raid alerts, the first duty of the police was to clear the streets. Once, after doing this, he retired to a building to which he had access, to what he thought in the darkness was a safe refuge under the stairs. Here he sat out the night, listening to the gunfire, and to occasional shell fragments clattering into the street. After some hours, a mysterious light began to glow round him, filtering down from above. Suddenly, he realised it was the dawn, and that he was sitting on the floor immediately under a large skylight.

A recurring activity was to deal with soldiers in London on brief leaves from the interminable trench warfare in France. Very often, and not very unnaturally, they were drunk. Dad was never known to arrest one. He always coaxed them to go with him to the Union Jack Club at Waterloo Station, or some hostel, where they could be cared for, and sleep it off. One of these gentlemen, an Australian, insisted on presenting him with the remains of a very large chunk of dark bitter chocolate which had come back with him from France. Dad brought it home. To sustain him on the journey, the soldier had nibbled it all over. It was a mass of toothmarks. However, chocolate was a rarity then. Mother took a sharp knife, shaved away all the toothmarks for hygiene's sake, and divided the central core amongst us children. Another man, however, was fighting drunk and it took five policemen to get him to a cell, to which he was taken strapped down to a wheeled stretcher.

I still have amongst my few souvenirs Dad's truncheon (which he never used), his red and white striped brassard or armlet, and the medal he was given after the war for long service.

There were difficulties and restrictions, but a surprising number of things went on unaffected. School was, I think, never interrupted. Even the routine medical examinations of the schoolchildren continued. I know that, for on one occasion I was one of a number of children who had their tonsils removed. This we had done at a clinic, and I for one was left quite terrified by the 'laughing gas' which put me to sleep, and the bleeding which continued chokingly in my throat for hours afterwards. My astigmatism was also identified by an eye-test. I got my first all-purpose spectacles, with frames of a silvery-looking wire, when I was nine years old in 1916, and I have had to wear glasses ever since.

I even sat my examination for Christ's Hospital during the war, and in May 1918, walked up the long avenue in the Sussex sunshine to draw from the stores the odd Tudor-style uniform of ankle-length blue coat, knee-breeches, and yellow stockings, and to embark on six years of boarding-school life. Here, too, the effect of the war was more of niggling detail than of a major pressure on our lives. It meant little to me when, each Sunday evening in chapel, the headmaster read out the names of the former pupils who had been reported killed that week. None of the names was known to me, and I could not picture someone choking in the cold Atlantic waters, or torn apart by a shellburst in the mud of the trenches. For me, the facts of war were that the food was uninteresting and repetitive. The main dish at our midday dinner three times a week was billed as 'stewed steak', 'Irish Stew', and 'Lancashire hotpot', but the difference between them was undetectable, and they were absorbed with a conscious effort, even by hungry boys. Sometimes instead of potatoes there would be a wet heap of boiled swedes. Bread, even, was measured out by cutting the loaves down the middle, and then crosswise at the punctures made by nails protruding regularly from wooden battens, to indicate four-ounce portions at breakfast and tea, and two-ounce portions at dinner.

Occasionally, too, some of us missed a class to be sent out into the fields to help a farmer, short of labourers, by potato-gleaning. A horse pulled a wheeled device called a 'kicker' which broke up the rows of plants, and was supposed to push the potatoes into a suspended bag. We followed behind to collect the fairly numerous tubers which were missed and left behind.

Why did that war have such a muted effect on me? First, I suppose, because I was shielded from it fairly systematically by my parents, schoolteachers and others, cosseted and cared for, and given the best of what was available. There was, too, a strong policy of 'business as usual' wherever this was possible. My wife remembers her father saying, 'The Kaiser can stop me from putting sugar in my tea, but he can't stop me from stirring it as if it was there.' Then, I am sure that there is a defence mechanism in the young, which insulates them to a great degree against the unpleasant and the unknown. It is not a complete defence, but often it means that the child is unaware of what is happening.

We British, too, have an attitude towards war and other major perils which is uncommon amongst other communities. The average Frenchman or German, if there is such a person, might consider it improper. It is irreverent, slightly mocking and yet deprecating. Here are three examples of it which all date from the war of 1914 to 1918.

Two are from *Punch,* the humorous weekly which is now a century old but can still raise a laugh sometimes. The first picture showed two soldiers on leave from France, shabby, battered, garlanded with weapons and equipment, their feet and legs still clotted with the mud of the trenches. One of them points out to the other Buckingham Palace in the background, with a squad of the Guards, immaculate in their bearskins and scarlet, precise in their drill. And he says: 'Look, Bill. Soldiers!'

The second was, I believe, drawn by Charles Graves, at the end of the war, long after the great naval battle referred to. On the deck of a battleship, an officer is glaring ferociously at an object which is being held upright by the mighty fist of a burly petty officer. It is just recognisably human, the face being hidden in a tangle of black hair and the body draped in the tatters of a seaman's uniform. Says the petty officer: 'Fahnd 'im in the scuppers, sir. 'E's bin 'iding there ever since Jutland.'

The third is a postcard of the period, drawn by Bruce Bairnsfather, whose standard characters made the whole country laugh throughout those years – 'Old Bill', the archetype of the private soldier, short and tubby, with a spiky moustache radiating from his upper lip, and his young friend Bert, taller, stooping, and with a cigarette always drooping from his mouth. This one shows Bert looking out through a hole in a ruined cottage, with the usual war wreckage around. A shell is about to hit the cottage near his head. The caption read:

'SITUATION SHORTLY VACANT

> 'In an old-fashioned house in France, an opening will shortly occur for a young man, with prospects of getting a rise.'

Whatever the reasons were, the war was for me largely confined to such trivialities as seven hens in the back garden. The headlines in the newspapers, which gave, even when censored, a fair picture of what was happening, had little impact on me. But there was no television to bring pictures of it all directly into our home, and not even 'wireless'. Even the cinema was in a very limited stage of development. Also, as it happened, none of my close relations became war casualties, so there were no family discussions of the disappearance of faces known to us.

How strange it now seems that such vast events were mere shadows to many children of my age! Some ten million people were violently killed. Large areas of Belgium and France, as well as Eastern Europe, were fought over and over until they were reduced to a sea of mud, stuffed with corpses. The great Russian Empire, much more industrially developed and integrated with western European industry than we now remember, collapsed into ruin after great numbers were killed in prolonged fighting against the Germans. Out of that wreckage there emerged into the world a powerful new force, that of revolutionary ideology.

The German war machine with its equally formidable armaments industry was eventually crushed. The allies enforced what can now be seen as an impossibly severe reparations policy, which was the main cause of the total breakdown of the German economy. This in turn prepared the way for National Socialism and the Second World War. France and the United Kingdom lost so many of their best young men as to be seriously weakened for the future. It may be that this was one reason why, thirty years later, the British and French Empires were (as some believe) prematurely and hastily dismembered, with tragic results in most of the countries which were catapulted into independence. The Americans, too, had such losses as to cause them largely to withdraw from world politics for many years, fearing a repetition of the tragedy.

Possibly the most destructive effect was one which no statistics could measure, the damage done to accepted standards of behaviour, both personal and corporate, by an all-out war of over four years. The stable decades before the war presented a picture of an ordered society. No one pretended all was right with it, but people knew where they were with it. People kept their place for generations, a place defined by class, occupation, and often by locality of residence and work. Churches and schools were mostly of a traditional kind, well known and understood, and the same could be said even of the arts and entertainment – at least, in general. All changes took place at a dignified pace.

In the war, millions of fathers, brothers and sons left their families for years. So did many daughters, sisters and mothers. And many never returned. The wounds to family life were deep. Little wonder that the war was followed by restless and wild behaviour, by revolutions, currency fluctuations, unemployment, disorder of all kinds.

And in the years in which this inundation of change was loosed on to the world, I mostly moved, intent only on the next small activity, from schoolroom to playing-field, from book to country footpath.

When peace was finally announced in 1919, the eight hundred boys of Christ's Hospital were marched out to the top of the nearby hill called Sharpenhurst. There we stood through formal celebrations of a bonfire and firework display. It rained in torrents, and we all got soaked. That mattered little. We took the weather as it came. Then we marched back to a specially lavish tea in the dining-hall, ending with a slab of rich fruit cake for each boy. Now, that really was important.

8

Christ's Hospital. 1918 to 1924

The first thing which had a personal impact on me at Christ's Hospital was the school uniform. The second was my shadow.

I had been put on to a specified train at London Bridge Station by my mother, possibly supported in a slightly absent-minded way by my father – I am not sure. I was in the clothes I usually wore for school, and carried a small attaché case with certain items the school had carefully specified on a printed form. They were extraordinarily few. I think they just comprised underwear, white handkerchiefs, slippers, a comb and toothbrush, and the clothes I would need for cricket, namely, a dark blue flannel blazer, grey flannel shorts, a white shirt, grey socks, and black rubber shoes which we called plimsolls and I believe Americans call sneakers. Even nightwear was provided by the school.

It was impressive to find that the school had its own railway station in Sussex, but the mile walk seemed a long way on that early summer day in May 1918. The last stretch had trees on each side; on our left were large three-storey buildings, and smaller houses with gardens stood on the right. Our first call was at the stores, where shelves and cupboards held a bewildering array of clothes. Coats and breeches were briskly held up against us by the custodian and slapped down on a counter to be folded. Shoes were smacked down by our feet with a curt 'try those'. In minutes each new boy acquired a weighty pile of stuff with which he tottered out into the sunlight. It was now, I think, that my shadow ... No, I must first say something about those extraordinary clothes.

First, we were proud to wear them, and I believe Christ's Hospital boys of today are equally proud. Indeed, now that the girls' and boys' schools have been merged, the girls have been equipped with a modified version of the same uniform. The main difference is a skirt in

64

place of breeches. And it is true that only minor modifications have been made from the uniforms supplied when the school was founded in 1552. They were then similar to the ordinary garb of apprentices in London city.

The coat was ankle length, close-fitting in the sleeve and down to the waist, and pleated and full in the skirt. It was made of a very heavy and close-woven woollen cloth, which kept out all but the most torrential rain. A row of eight silvery-looking buttons fastened the front of the tunic, each bearing the bust of King Edward VI in relief. Inside (and out of sight), the upper part was lined with a bright yellow frieze. I believe that this dated back to when it was believed that the yellow colour kept away insects and infection.

Below it there were black breeches, again with three metal buttons at each knee. Below that again were the famous yellow stockings, of stout wool. When new, they were a rich orange-yellow, but with repeated washing they gradually faded to lemon. We arrived just after the school had given up the traditional shoes with a bright metal buckle. We were among the first to wear ordinary black lace-up shoes.

Under the coat we wore a collarless, buttonless shirt. The bands, which were worn one above the other at the neck, were on a strip of cotton or linen, which was pinned to the shirt at the back of the neck by a safety pin. A second safety pin in the front held together the two top corners of the shirt and the two ends of the strip carrying the bands. It took quite a knack to affix the pin under one's chin in such a way that all four layers were in alignment, and the twin bands fell neatly down the front of one's coat, over the top button.

These garments constituted our all-seasons, all-weather wear, with the sole addition of a waistcoat in winter – now, I believe, replaced by a pullover. Scarves and hats were forbidden. Gloves were considered to be for weaklings only, though it was permitted to walk with hands inside two slits in the coat in cold weather. If the weather was extremely hot, there would perhaps be an announcement by the powers that be that the coat could be replaced by the dark blue jacket, or blazer, for classes, for meals in hall, and generally.

And now the shadow. Each new boy was assigned a slightly older boy, termed his 'shadow', to look after him for his first month, see he got to the right class-rooms and so on, and instruct him in some of the basics in communal school living. I enquired not long ago if this system still operated at the school. It does, but the term 'shadow' has been replaced by 'nurse-maid'. I prefer the old title.

School uniform provided few problems. The chief one was to get one's bands in alignment, and the basic way to learn this was to keep practising until they could be pinned in a couple of seconds with eyes shut. Lack of experience cither left the two long tabs at weird angles, which made the boy look most eccentric, or (if combined with clumsiness) crumpled or dirtied the bands, which, being such a focal point of one's appearance, converted a cherubic child into a young tramp very quickly indeed.

There were, however, two hazards for new boys in connection with the coat. Walking slowly in a heavy ankle-length coat tends to an upright and elegant movement. If one walks fast, however, there is a tendency for the folds of the skirt to collect between the knees, and the novice can even be tripped up by this. The cure is a knack of swinging each knee slightly outwards as it comes forward, to 'knee' the coat a little to one side. The knack is quickly acquired. I think it stays with most of us, which accounts for the fact that sons of the school tend to walk a little like a sailing vessel running before the wind.

The second pitfall, in my time at any rate, was the level at which one wore one's girdle. Boys in the lower school were belted about outside their coats by a 'narrowie' girdle, an ordinary leather strap and buckle. On moving up the middle school, each boy achieved a 'broadie', a strap a good inch in width, fastened by a rather beautifully worked oval buckle in solid silver. This buckle had to be paid for at the impressive price of seven shillings and sixpence in 1919, when I went up from the Junior Fourth to the Lower Fourth. Lower-school and middle-school boys wore their girdles level with the seam around the bottom of the tunic part of the coat. Upper-school boys could wear them a few inches lower. Grecians and deputy Grecians (the two top forms bore these names, as for centuries before) could wear their girdles as low as they liked.

And woe, woe, to a boy who wore his girdle, even by accident, lower than his status permitted. Any senior observing this was not only liable to give him a tongue-lashing, but might also deliver suitable punishment. The simplest and most likely was an 'owl', the vigorous rap of knuckles one or more times to the crown of the head. It was quite painful.

The shadow's main duty, however, was to escort his charge to the class-room he should be in at any time, to the dining-hall for meals, and everywhere else he needed to be at various times in that first baffling month. He had, also, to explain a fairly extensive code of local rules and laws, some laid down by authority, and some by the boys themselves. There were areas where a boy might only go at certain times, and areas where he might never go. And there was also 'Housey slang'. The school was informally referred to as Housey, or, as some said it used to be spelt, Housie. And in my time you would be in trouble if you did not use the recognised school expressions, many of which had been in use for ages. Edmund Blunden, the poet, in his book on Christ's Hospital, records a couple of pages of 'Housey slang', such as 'brown' for a penny, 'kiff' for tea, 'crug' for bread, and 'spadge' for a stroll. It was still in use in my time, as it was in the days of Coleridge and Lamb about 1790. Sadly, it is dying out now. Perhaps it has already gone. But if I referred to 'bread' or 'tea' in my first days at school, I would be met with a blank look, or possibly an 'owl'. And my shadow would lose face, too.

The boy assigned as my shadow was Laborde, son of a naval officer. After he left the school, he went to New Zealand and became a farmer. When I met him in 1918, he was a stocky, round-faced boy who, unlike myself, was bursting with self-confidence. He had had a year or two in the preparatory school, and a couple of terms, perhaps, in the main school.

The school itself was a huge group of structures in red brick, still very new, since the ancient foundation had only moved to Sussex from central London sixteen years before. Its grounds seemed vast to a London boy. Later, I calculated that there were over twenty rugby football pitches, and over thirty cricket pitches, besides fives courts, a gymnasium, indoor swimming bath, and much else. The big central quadrangle and cloisters included the chapel, dining-hall and the speech hall for major functions (always known as 'Big School'). The class-rooms were set round it, and the boarding-houses in which we lived and slept lined the north side of the main avenue, curving away on both sides of the quad. The houses were in pairs. The easternmost pair was the preparatory school for boys from about nine to eleven – known as Prep.A and Prep.B. The others were all named after honoured old boys; from east to west they were Maine, Barnes (an early editor of the London *Times*), Lamb (essayist), Coleridge (poet), Middleton (first Anglican Bishop of Calcutta), Thornton (a diplomat) and Peele (another poet). Who was Maine? A lawyer, I think, and a writer about law. I was in Middleton B. Each house held fifty boys, except the prep., which held sixty each. With masters and their families, and everybody else, the whole community must have been some twelve hundred or so.

The first time I scurried across the quad with my shadow, Laborde pointed out the fountain in the centre, topped with a statue in lead of the boy king, Edward VI. 'The founder,' he explained, 'fifteen fifty-two.' I heard the story later, how, after Henry VIII had quarrelled with the Pope and set up an independent English church, he dissolved the monasteries and appropriated their possessions. Since the monasteries included in their activities the relief of the poor and sick, these unfortunates were largely left uncared for. Ridley, the Bishop of London, preached a challenging sermon on this issue in St. Paul's Cathedral before the young King Edward, the mayor, sheriffs and aldermen of the City of London. Edward, though sickly and shortly to die, summoned the mayor, aldermen and merchants afterwards, and asked them what they proposed to do. As a result, they founded three 'hospitals', St Thomas's for the sick, Christ's for the children running wild in the streets, and Bethlehem Hospital for those without homes or work. The last became in later years the infamous 'Bedlam' for the insane. Christ's Hospital was built, by a sort of justice, on the site of one of the monasteries Henry seized. He had promised the land for some charitable purpose.

Still, after four hundred years, the school is dedicated to the service of children who need care and education. Those most in need are clothed, boarded and educated free. The parents and guardians of those in less acute need are called on to make some contribution to the cost. My father paid thirty pounds a year: that was much more in those distant years than it is today – for much of his life, Dad never earned more than four hundred pounds a year – but it meant that our financial benefit from the school was great. And my brother Don joined the school too, when I left. He even took over my 'permanent number'. All his clothes, like mine, were marked 'Mid.B 18'. His shoes were in pigeon-hole 18 overnight, and his sports clothes on peg number 18.

Well, back to my shadow. My relationship with him was a somewhat prickly one. I was coping with loneliness, fear of the unknown, and a feeling of inferiority with not much success, and sometimes tried to compensate for it by resisting pressure from anyone – which usually meant Laborde. This made him brusque and irritable. At one point we came to blows. I don't know how it developed, but others intervened, and somehow I found myself committed to a fight with him behind the fives courts after morning school. By some means news of this reached my housemaster, who could have banned the fight, but elected instead to say that if we wanted to fight, we should do it in a proper civilised manner, with a referee to supervise. So a few hours later we met in the dormitory with a few spectators, a set of boxing gloves were produced, and beds were pushed around to make a primitive ring. We took off our coats. The housemaster himself was referee and timekeeper, and I think we fought five two-minute rounds. Laborde stood no nonsense from me, and pummelled my ribs in a way which left me sore for days. I was not so strong or skilled, but I did manage to land a punch which made his nose bleed. On the strength of this, the match was declared a draw. As to whether this was a civilised procedure for eleven-year-olds, opinions may differ, but at least we could live together after it. And did.

J.W.F. Forbes, our senior housemaster (two masters lived in each house), was only one of many slightly eccentric characters amongst the teaching staff. The bulk of them had been at the school since the move from London in 1902, and some for longer still. He was a big man with a heavy moustache, loose tweedy clothes (over which, of course, he wore a black gown to and in class), and a bald head, sun-browned like leather. He walked with a pronounced limp. The explanation for this amongst the boys was that when mountain-climbing in the holidays 'he fell off an Alp'. He taught mathematics, mostly to middle forms, teaching well but in a slightly off-hand or absent-minded way. He was only a moderate man for discipline, certainly not unduly strict. And he possessed two vehicles which were a constant source of mild amusement. One was a heavy bicycle. It had a fixed step, a bar extending the back axle, and he invariably set out in the same way. He grasped the handlebars, put his left foot on the step, and pushed away with the right leg until he had momentum enough to swing the leg over the saddle. With his awkward lame leg, his prominent behind, and the black gown floating in the breeze, it was always a popular spectacle. His other means of transport was a Trojan car. Cars were not so common in 1918, but the Trojan was so basic that it would make today's Citroën 2CV look like a luxury limousine. It was a two-seater with, I think, a two-stroke engine. At any rate, it sounded like one. And it had disc wheels and narrow solid rubber tyres. Altogether, it was a very primitive form of motoring, noisy, slow and uncomfortable.

He strongly supported our sports teams, though it was alleged that he knew nothing about sport. At rugby football matches against other houses, he would always be on the touchline, shouting encouragement. It was, however, rumoured that his tactical advice was always the same. Whenever our side was running with the ball, Forbes always shouted, 'Make for the corner!' A slander, no doubt.

Perhaps the best index to his character was in his attitude to punishment, in those days when corporal punishment in boys' schools was taken for granted, and was sometimes fairly brutal. His resort to the cane always seemed to me to be reluctant. It was the accepted method, and sometimes he felt it was his duty to use it. He used it on me three times in six years. The first time was the only occasion when I felt that he really laid on with conviction. It was for swearing at a monitor, and I think Forbes wanted to be sure that for me it should be 'never again'. In that disciplined school, such a combination of temper and foul language could not be tolerated. I had to bend over the back of an armchair and grasp the edge of the seat to provide a good taut target, and got 'six of the best'. When I was drying myself at the swimming bath next day, Forbes came past, took my shoulder and turned me round for a second so that he could see the result of his strokes. He made no comment, but must have been satisfied. There was no blood, and only three weals from six strokes. Good accurate work, and no excess about it.

The second occasion was farcical. We had two brothers in the house named Tandy. Their sister Jessica Tandy eventually became a famous actress, and both the boys were interested in the stage. A.H. (ultimately to become British ambassador to the European Community) took the name part when Rostand's *Cyrano de Bergerac* was staged at the school, and later took an active part in the Oxford University Dramatic Society. The younger brother E.J., who became a marine engineer, conceived an ambitious project when he was still only a junior, say twelve or thirteen years old. He wrote a melodrama, directed its production, and starred in it himself, even writing in a piccolo solo for himself, since he played this instrument in the school orchestra. It was eventually staged with official approval in the junior dormitory for the whole house. However, before this was achieved, we had several rehearsals, also in the dorm. The cast were all juniors. I had a minor part as the heroine's father. At one rehearsal, we lost track of time until six o'clock struck, and the bell went for tea, the last meal of the day. We grabbed our coats and fled, leaving the dormitory strewn with props, including rugs from the beds used as curtains, a sheet used as a table-cloth, and several towels used for swaddling my 'gouty' leg. In our absence at tea, matron discovered the mess, and made a Very Serious Complaint. Forbes paraded the whole cast outside his study, all ten of us, and gave us a token two taps of the cane each.

The third occasion, which was when I quite accidentally pulled the communication cord as some colleagues were trying to put me on to the luggage rack of the special train taking us to London, was also an occasion when the caning was not much more than symbolic. He gave me six strokes of the cane, but there was no conviction or weight behind them. The railway company duly wrote a terrifying letter, pointing out that the penalty under the bye-laws was the vast sum of five pounds. Forbes took it away to answer on my behalf. A few days later, just before lights out, he came up to my bed. 'Ho, Ledwith. I've heard from the railway company. What about that five pounds, eh?' Pause. 'Well, I told them I'd given you a good beating, and they say that was much the best way to deal with it.' I was speechless with relief.

The proof of Forbes' nature, however, is that when he retired, some years after I left, many former boys of his house organised a dinner in his honour, and made a presentation to him. I was there. And many kept in touch with him for years after. He bought a house a mile from the school, and all were welcome to drop in on him there.

Were the masters generally as eccentric as we thought they were? Perhaps. More likely, we seized on, repeated to each other, and exaggerated every characteristic we noted. There were those who barked at us, those who stammered, those who made jokes. There was the Reverend L.H. White, who ran the Natural History Society and was therefore 'Buggy' White. He had a glass eye, and would fix you with one eye, while the other glared out of the window. There was the vivacious Henri Bué, who taught French. One wall of his class-room was covered by a huge poster of French troops involved in an exciting battle. In the foreground was a life-sized infantryman in kepi, blue coat with the skirts folded back, and red trousers, with his rifle and fixed bayonet. To the soldier's elbow Bué had fixed with a drawing-pin a card bearing the motto: 'Don't keep your wishbone where your backbone ought to be.' He was a keen amateur photographer, too, and once, regardless of discipline, showed some of us a snapshot taken at the school sports, during a close contest for the high jump. Three masters, oblivious to everything except the boy clearing the bar, were standing in a row with their mouths wide open. Each, in sympathy with the jumper's effort, had lifted one leg high in the air. Bué was also a considerable scholar. His textbooks on French for schools were highly regarded, and (though I did not know this until long after I left school) he had translated *Alice in Wonderland* into French. That, I should imagine, would test any translator to breaking point.

There was E.C. Wright, man of many parts, housemaster, hall

warden (keeping eight hundred boys in order in the dining-hall at all meals), and coach of the school cricket teams. He was known as 'Brushy' on account of his alleged constant use of the cane. Certainly, he had to punish those who misbehaved in hall in addition to the 'crimes' which all masters had to keep down, but it was surely untrue that he used the occasions to practise his cricket strokes, such as the square cut. A.E. Johnson, one of the science masters, was always called 'Ganot' because of his faith in the textbook on physics by that author. His staccato 'Look-it-up-in-Ganot' was always being imitated. And so it went on.

I experienced two headmasters at Christ's Hospital. My first year was also the last of the long rule of Dr Upcott, a white-bearded, aloof figure always in clerical dress. He never spoke to me, and was reported not to speak to any boys except Grecians. The impression he gave was of undiluted remoteness and severity. However, I have since realised that I only knew the last worn-out days of a good headmaster. And one factor I never realised at all at the time was the strain on him of the years of war, and of the almost daily news of premature death striking down his former pupils. What were meaningless names to me in those lists read out in chapel, brought to him mental pictures of youths he had known for years, had cherished, and for whom he had had great hopes.

His successor, W. Hamilton Fyfe, eventually Sir William, was a very different kind of man, warm and approachable. I will not dwell on his later career in universities in Canada and Scotland, but only sketch how he appeared to me. He, too, could be severe. Once he came to the dining-hall rostrum to make an announcement – a rare phenomenon. It was brief. 'Reports have been made to me that some boys have been what they call scrumping. I call it stealing apples from farmers. This – must – stop.' The words cracked like a whip. And he stepped down.

He and Mrs Fyfe would have small groups of boys of any age to tea with them at weekends. He took an interest in everything that went on. Of course, with eight hundred boys, this meant that most of us rarely had personal contact with him. In fact, I heard him say that a maximum of six hundred would give him a better chance to know everybody. My own contacts with him were few.

On one occasion, three of us went to him for permission to be out of school for a whole day for some special purpose. He listened, agreed, and signed a pass for us. Then he said, 'You'll need some food to take with you. Show this to the Lady Superintendent of the kitchens.' He wrote a second note, and gave it to us in an unsealed envelope. As soon as we were outside, we read the note, as no doubt he expected. It said: 'Miss Blank. Please give these beasts a nosebag. W.H.F.' To us, familiar with the sight of the greengrocer's or coal merchant's horse champing in his nosebag full of straw while deliveries were being made, it was delightful, if also slightly deflationary to youthful self-importance.

When I was in an upper form, probably those Deputy Grecians specialising in mathematics, the headmaster arranged with our English master that he should read, mark and discuss our English essays once or twice a term. This was always a treat. He would come in, in his plain black gown over a green tweed suit, thump down the pile of twenty-odd essays on the desk, perch gold-rimmed glasses on his long nose, and launch straight into criticism. But this could lead into all sorts of subjects which flowed out of the things we had been told to write about. We never knew what would come up next – quotations from a wide range of writers, reminiscence, discussion of style or the origins of words, challenges to accepted dicta of the time. He could be terse, too. The worse the essay, the briefer the comment. He picked up one paper, read the author's name off the top, and said, 'Yes. Yumour (as he pronounced it) is all very well when it's yumorous. When it's not, it's the very devil.'

After I left Christ's Hospital, I never went near the school for eight years. Then, one day, I cycled down to Horsham and, by sheer chance, encountered Fyfe in the cloisters. He was about to pass by with a 'good morning', but stopped in mid-stride and turned back to say, 'Ledwith, isn't it? Mid.B. You went into business, didn't you?' Not bad after an eight years' gap, with someone he'd maybe spoken to three or four times before.

I am trying to sort out from a myriad of memories, some dim, some crystal clear, the factors which influenced me in after life, which affected my character, my outlook, and the course of events. They were not always the obvious things, the daily services in chapel with the organ booming, or the pageantry of Speech Day, when the Lord Mayor of London came in state each year with attendant sheriffs, and senior boys gave orations in Latin and English. (When the first Elizabeth came to the throne, and made her progress through London, the children of Christ's Hospital greeted her, with a brilliant Latin oration by young Edmund Campion; later in her reign, he was to be executed by her authority when he returned covertly as a Jesuit priest. In those turbulent days, any Catholic was suspected to be a spy or agent of Catholic Spain.) They were, too, not necessarily the basic training the school gave to mind and body, thorough though this was in class-room and playing-field. And they were not the occasional exciting incident, as when Edward, Prince of Wales landed on a cricket pitch in a light aeroplane, did a quick tour, publicly asked for and obtained a half-holiday for us, and disappeared again.

I think more of such incidents as my first Sunday afternoon at the school in May, 1918. Laborde, usually so effectively my shadow, forgot to tell me the routine, when for at least two hours after one o'clock dinner we were forbidden the house and had to find something to do outside. A monitor found me in the deserted day-room, and drove me out. I had no friends, little idea what was permitted or not permitted, and if I wandered far I feared getting lost. It was a hot, still afternoon. I drifted round to the front of Middleton B, where a few senior boys were basking in the sun on the lawn, writing letters or reading. I dared not speak to them. I had neither writing paper, nor a book. Two of them, sharing a rug and reading peacefully were (though I did not know them, of course) friends and frequent companions. One was L.D. Smith, the elder of two brothers, rather tall, bespectacled, with a jerky manner of speech and movement. A classical scholar, he eventually had a distinguished career in the law, mostly in distant parts of the world. Forty years later, a paper landed on my desk in my London office, an order issued in respect of a shipping dispute at Tarakan in Borneo. I looked at the signature, and looked again. The judge who had issued the order was L.D. Smith. The second person was a smaller fellow, compactly built, with yellow hair. I later knew him as a dashing batsman at cricket. He concentrated on engineering studies later, and became a civil engineering consultant. His name was Fry, Sidney Eustace Fry, I seem to remember, which is strange, for we almost never used Christian names at school.

They saw me looking lost and miserable, and spoke to me. The reason being established, one of them said, 'Well, you read this. We'll read to each other.' He handed over his book (was it a Rider Haggard novel?), and they took turns in reading aloud from the other.

It was a trifling incident. Yet the graciousness and sensitivity of it are still bright to me today.

Fry figured in another incident, but it was pure coincidence that I was involved too. It could have been any junior. Some months later, taking advantage of the cover given him by the bustle and confusion in the dining-hall, a great lout of a boy in the next house to ours kicked me savagely. It was the sort of wanton, purposeless brutality which occasionally appears amongst boys. The next moment, the bully found a figure in front of him, tensely erect, though he was half a head shorter in height. In a flash, Fry delivered what we called a 'fotch' (also used as a punishment), a round-armed swing with the flat hand on the side of his face, hard enough to make him stagger. Fry spat some words at him in a low voice. I expect it was, 'You leave our juniors alone.' The massive brute cowered away, and scrambled back into his seat, even his neighbours in his own house turning away from him. I never saw him terrorise a junior again.

Games played a big part at Christ's Hospital. In my time there, they were the biggest single factor in establishing one's personal status, though numerous factors could be important. Games will be dealt with in the next chapter, but this one might well conclude by looking at Christ's Hospital in a broader context.

At the time I was there it was the second biggest boarding-school in England. Only Eton had more boys as boarders. What was more important was that it was an example of almost all the advantages of the independent boarding-schools which we English have long referred to illogically as 'public schools', but without their disadvantages. Perhaps for 'disadvantages' one should put 'the features for which the independent schools are most criticised'.

There has probably been more controversy over the independent schools in recent decades than over any other aspect of education in the United Kingdom. Some of it applies to those day schools usually called 'grammar schools', as well as to the 'public schools'. Some of each group are schools of ancient foundation, going back to centuries when education was the privilege of the few, confined to those intended for government and the church, and to a lesser extent the merchant class. Both groups, however, have been enlarged greatly century by century, as new schools have been added, sometimes by public bodies, sometimes through the funds of private benefactors.

The 1944 Education Act made possible extensive reforms, not least of which was the chance to integrate the grammar schools into the state system of secondary education, now to be available for all children. The grammar schools could and generally did become 'direct grant' schools, whereby public funds became available to them, but they retained, in general, their independence. The public schools were not much affected. Local education authorities could pay to send individual children to the independent boarding-schools but these powers were only used to a limited degree.

Later, a more left-wing government did away with the 'direct grant' system, the grammar schools having to choose between being fully integrated into the state system, controlled and financed by the local education authorities, or forgoing any grants in order to keep their independence. Some did one thing, some the other.

At frequent intervals in recent years plans have been put forward to abolish or take over the 'public schools', so that they too would come wholly into the state system. In the case of the more extreme proponents of these schemes, the motive is very much of a class nature, and the argument is based on the supposed immorality of some children being given a better education than others. A larger and more moderate group of critics, however, argue that a few hundred schools charging high fees are a bad influence on the general situation of education in the country, because they can afford to draw away the best teachers, and thus limit the opportunities for the children of the general body of families, which cannot afford the high fees. It is also argued that it is bad for children to be segregated in a school confined to one class of person.

Proponents of the public schools not only point to their long history, and their record of scholarship and effective training in other ways. They also say that there should be freedom for parents to choose what schools their children attend, and claim that an increasing number of families want the system to continue, even at great financial sacrifice by parents. The system, too, seems to be copied more and more in other countries, including India, Nigeria and, it is said, the USSR.

Like most far-reaching arguments, there is a good deal to be said for both points of view – which are of course only crudely sketched in here. Christ's Hospital, as mentioned, is something which breaks the general pattern. Its governors seek to give the children an education and facilities equal to the finest of the independent schools. Yet it is certainly not a school for the privileged. Normally, it is impossible for a child to be admitted unless the parents are in need of financial help with its education. The fees are nominal and may be waived entirely. Recently, it was decided that children and grandchildren of former scholars could be admitted on payment of the full cost, notwithstanding that their parents' financial standing was above the fairly low level applied as a criterion, but such instances are still rare. Thus, there is a very wide mixture of social backgrounds amongst the boys and girls. When I was there, a fair proportion seemed to be the children of country clergy or junior officers in the fighting services – both lowly paid professions. A couple of years ago, the Senior

Grecian told me that the big change in his seven or eight years in the school was the increase in the number of those from single-parent homes. These are not necessarily produced by divorce or separation: the situation can equally arise from the death of one parent, from serious illness, or from a long prison sentence. And this is an area in society where severe need is most likely.

In comparison, I recall our consulting the head of one of the top girls' public schools about our daughter's future. She was quite eager to have her, as coming from a settled home background, partly because so many of her girls came from broken homes, or from parents living and working abroad, who could give little home life in the holidays. Also, she said, some families were so rich that a child's every wish was automatically met, for a pony, a yacht, or whatever. Some of these families, she said, undid during every holiday all that the school tried to do for the girls each term. We would have done without many things to send our daughter to such a school if it had seemed right. However, after much thought, the right place seemed to be a 'direct grant' grammar school not far from our home.

Do the public schools perpetuate the class system, and produce a type of person unsuitable for the kind of society we want to see? I find it hard to answer this with a direct 'no' or 'yes'. Perhaps they do produce a certain number of snobs, narrow-minded, unpleasant to people they consider to be their inferiors, and unable to comprehend things outside the small world of 'people like them'. But I feel that this is basically a question of character, not of schooling. In the City, I mixed intimately with many from what are usually considered the topmost and 'most exclusive' public schools, but equally with many from all sorts of other backgrounds. Both groups include good men, and less good. Just before I wrote this passage, I attended an occasion to honour a long-time City friend. His father was a lighterman on the Thames. The function was a grand affair, and a peer proposed my friend's health. The four senior partners of the firm I worked in, covering the sixty years I have known the firm, had their secondary education respectively at the Royal Naval College, Dartmouth, at Winchester, at a north London secondary school, and at Eton.

Perhaps the question behind this question is the more important one: 'What is the aim of education?' But I am not going to try to answer that! Who would? An educational newspaper offered a small prize for the best answer in a few hundred words. The winner's entry was excellent, and thought-provoking, but it was the only entry. And it came from India.

Perhaps, too, it may help to think for a moment of the kind of person one school has produced. In that kaleidoscope of personalities it is hard to see any pattern. However, from Christ's Hospital in the years since I was there, some notable figures have emerged, and many more who have made worthy but modest contributions. The fact that none of them had money or influence behind him may have helped to decide how they developed, many of them as administrators, accountants, company secretaries, the people who keep things running. There have been several top civil servants, but only one Cabinet Minister (Michael Stewart). There have been doctors, including Brock, the heart surgeon. There have been many middle-rank insurance men, and one chairman of the Sun Life Office. Barnes Wallis, engineer and perhaps the most fertile inventor of the century, was before my time, but active in school affairs throughout the period. Middleton Murry the writer was earlier, too, but since then we have had Bernard Levin the controversial, writing in *The Times*. Musicians include Constant Lambert, composer, William Glock of the BBC, and Colin Davis, conductor. There have been good soldiers and naval men, but none prominent, except a Chaplain-General to the forces. And so it goes on. I can take a certain pride in being an inconspicuous figure in that crowd, and so it could be with any school.

I have had plenty of evidence in my own contacts that the public schools, with their long traditions, stubbornly maintained, do produce citizens of merit, and quite often of outstanding merit. If this situation were to be destroyed, the nation would lose much. If indeed they provide a better preparation for life than other schools, as even some of their critics allege, the answer is surely to be sought in trying to bring the other schools up to their standards, not to drag everyone down to the lowest level. The pursuit of excellence is not a question of class. It should be part of everyone's make-up, whether scientist, mother, statesman, craftsman or whatever. When I was a filing clerk, I tried to make the firm's filing better than it had ever been before – this at a time when what I learnt at school was fresh in my mind.

Christ's Hospital, despite its unique status (proudly flaunted by the equally unique school uniform), had and I believe still has contacts in many ways with the 'public schools'. When we were matched with them in sporting, academic or other ways, we met them as equals. Sometimes we won in such contests, and sometimes we lost. But we were not really interested as to whether Housey was as good as, or even better than, the fee-paying schools. We were content to be what we were, and that the school should be judged on its merits.

Christ's Hospital is widely recognised as unusual, especially in the survival to an extreme degree of its charitable purpose of helping those in need. One scholar described it as 'sui generis'. Since my time, the school has changed in many ways. A second range of science laboratories has been built. There are extended facilities for music, and a purpose-built, fully-equipped theatre. Better and more varied sporting facilities are provided. The biggest change, in 1985, was to move down the girls' school from Hertford and merge it with the boys' school. Adjustments were made, to provide for six hundred boys, and two hundred girls. The four boarding-houses for girls each contain pupils from the whole range of ages, but some of the boys' houses are for younger boys only, and the others for their elders. The move was carefully considered before it was effected. In fact, it is said that it was first proposed in 1880!

Many of the independent schools in Britain have special characteristics. There are Catholic schools of great distinction, such as Ampleforth and Downside. Others have strong Protestant traditions, Anglican, Methodist (like Kingswood) and of the Society of Friends. Some, including Wellington, have a long connection with the armed services. Others have a special interest in a particular sport or sports, or in particular branches of study. Hundreds of families insist that their children should go to some individual school, generation after generation, and at great financial sacrifice, because that school has a character which they respect above all others.

On the evidence, my judgement is that we should welcome the fact that our country has such a variety of different schools, and that all of them should be encouraged to pursue excellence in education in their varying ways.

9

Games and holidays. 1918 to 1924

Games were important at Housey, or C.H., as it was sometimes called. Cricket and rugby football were compulsory for all boys, also swimming, gymnasium, rifle shooting with a standard Lee-Enfield service rifle lined to take a small-bore bullet, and cross-country running. Athletics and fives were officially encouraged, though not compulsory. And for part of my time at the school, we also had outdoor physical training of the usual bending and stretching kind for ten minutes a day. We tended to resent having to change into sports things for this brief interlude, either before breakfast or at the mid-morning break. It was understood to be a fad of the school doctor, who also tended to experiment, usually successfully, with our diet.

It looks quite a programme when set out, and of course it did represent a fixed policy to fill our time out of class with physical activity, as far as possible, six days a week. We were in class six mornings a week for nearly three hours, and four afternoons for an hour and a half. Wednesdays and Saturdays, when there were no afternoon classes, were always used for cricket in the summer term or rugby football in the other terms, and on the other afternoons from, say, four to six o'clock, there would be more of the same, or the other activities mentioned.

To go into the question of organised games would be a bore, especially by someone like myself whose level of achievement in the various sports was in the lower strata, from rather poor to deplorable. However, there were some valuable aspects even for less effective participants. One was the social discipline of regular, indeed constant, team games. You had to learn to be one of a team, or else life was unbearable. The other was also enforced by circumstances, the study of how to endure, and even get amusement from adverse circumstances.

80

Rugby football, for example, was played in any weather. Sometimes, it is true, it would be on dry turf, with a cool breeze and a bright sky. Yet I remember one game I played in on a notoriously muddy pitch. It was very cold, but not freezing, and it rained. The ball (a leather one, not plastic, in those days) quickly became sodden, heavy and covered with a film of liquid mud. It was quite impossible to handle it with any certainty, to pass it from hand to hand, or indeed to kick it any distance. Even if you tried to hold the ball and run with it, it slipped out of your fingers, or else you slipped in the mud yourself and fell down. Within minutes of the start we were all plastered solid with mud from head to foot. Yet merriment rose amongst us, and grew steadily throughout the match. Partly, this was because we assessed the peculiar conditions more quickly than our opponents did, and adapted our tactics accordingly. They kept on trying to handle the ball, only to drop it, or to kick it a long distance, only to fall flat on their backs. This alone was quite diverting. We worked out that the only way to make progress was to give the ball as it lay on the mud an almighty kick. This caused it to slide up to ten or twenty feet towards the other side's goal line. The quickest way to reach the ball again was not to try to run in an orthodox manner. The foothold was not good enough for that. One had to slide alternate feet on the mud in an action something like roller-skating and something like ski-ing. On reaching the ball, another hefty kick (if one didn't over-balance) would gain a few more yards. So we won, and that was funnier still.

As evidence of the truth of this story I will state that I had borrowed someone else's boots for this game. They were too small, and they rubbed the skin off my toes, but I enjoyed the game so much that I did not realise this had happened until the game was over. The walk back to the house was agonising.

Another game was played in a snowstorm, with a couple of inches of snow on the ground. At every opportunity, we forwards formed a scrum and kept the ball in as long as possible, so that we could cling together for warmth. The half-backs and three-quarters kept shouting 'Have it out!' while we called to each other, 'Keep it in.' The master refereeing the match was the coldest of all, and he cut the length of the first half to twenty minutes. We changed ends. The snow continued, and after another five minutes, he blew the whistle for 'time'.

With all this activity, day after day, it might be thought that we got a surfeit of games. In point of fact, a lot of energy was also expended in other, unofficial games. We even had a few enthusiasts for association football in Middleton B, who would try to get twenty-two boys together on a rare free afternoon to play by that code, which was officially regarded as inferior. More commonly, our unofficial games were quickly organised and briskly played in the odd half-hour or hour between other activities, say between the end of class, and parading for dinner.

Pride of place must, I think, go to asphalt soccer, for which all you needed was an old tennis ball and some boys, arbitrarily split into two teams. There was an area of asphalt between each pair of houses and the adjoining pair which was spacious enough for the purpose. The goal at each end was the wall between two designated drainpipes. We folded back the skirts of our coats, tucked the folded ends into our girdles, and set to. One boy roughly my age added a twist of his own to these games. He was very tall, and with unusually big feet. When, as I described earlier, we were fitted with lace-up shoes, there were none available for this size, and he had to accept a pair of the old buckled shoes. If a high ball came to him in asphalt soccer, he would take a swing at it, and the buckled shoe would come off, and soar high in the air. With a cry of 'Heads under!' both teams would scatter, until the shoe crashed to earth, and we could resume.

A variant to this was asphalt hockey. This again used a tennis ball. The 'sticks' we used were ash walking-sticks. Rough ones could be bought for a few pence, or even cut in the woods. The pitch and goals and general atmosphere were the same as for asphalt soccer. And in summer we would of course play asphalt cricket, again with a tennis ball. Wickets were chalked on the wall, and old cricket bats had their sides planed away in the Manual School (where we did woodwork, metalwork and other crafts) until they were what we called 'broomsticks'.

There were day-room sports, too. The day-room occupied almost the whole of the front of the house. It had windows on three sides, and a glassed partition on the fourth side, where double doors gave on to the main transverse passage which went across both Middleton B and Middleton A. This great room was deserted during the teaching periods and during organised games, but at other times it seethed with all kinds of activities.

In the evenings it was quiet, while we did our 'prep', the equivalent of a day-school's homework, on four or five long heavy tables, arranged crosswise in the room with benches on each side. During these periods the older boys were at the table farthest from the doors, the others ranging downwards in age table by table. Two tiny studies at the remotest corners gave a degree of privacy to the house captain and his second in command, and there were small tables at the sides where the other monitors kept a watchful eye.

One of these tables was taken over by the senior housemaster once a week, so that he could give out pocket-money. Each boy went up to the table, and said how much he wanted to draw. The recommended sum for parents to lodge with the housemaster was ten shillings a term. Out of this we were supposed to finance a weekly letter home, so one would tend to say, 'Sixpence and a three-ha'penny stamp, please, sir', or something like that. This would be doled out, and an entry made in his big book.

But during the day, between the fixed framework of hours set aside for classes, games, and meals, all kinds of things happened in the day-room, which was constantly astir. Two or three of us even attempted to mount a play-reading in German on one occasion, thinking (rightly) that we did not have enough opportunity in class to speak the language. But you must imagine up to fifty boys in the big room, miscellaneously occupied in almost any indoor pursuit of males between eleven and eighteen. Talking and reading went on all the time, chess, draughts, stamp-collecting, and much else.

Two variants of well-known games were among the noisier activities. The rules were, I think, the recognised rules, but the equipment was improvised to suit the peculiar conditions. Nowadays, there are plenty of people who say loud and long that every child has a right of access to the finest possible equipment for all the sports dreamt up by man, to Olympic standard swimming-pools, athletic tracks, and so on and so on. Do they forget the immense pleasure to be had from improvisation? Some of the greatest test cricketers in the world first learnt their skills in an Australian back street, or on a West Indian beach.

Billiards was one popular game in our day-room. Once people had been persuaded to vacate one of the tables, improvisation quickly provided the rest. There was no impeccably smooth green cloth cover. The surface was of deal, with the natural grain of the wood emphasised into ridges by constant digging with pencils and other implements by boys deep in thought over their prep. The size, too, was not standard, being more like fifteen feet by three. The side cushions were made by tipping two benches against each side, so that the backs projected some two inches above the table top. The end cushions were bound volumes of *Punch* laid flat on the table. Pockets were simply gaps between the benches and the books, so that balls potted or sent 'in off' had to be pursued across the floor among a welter of legs and furniture. The balls themselves were old fives balls, one of the three having a couple of dabs of red ink to identify it. The cues were a couple of the ash walking-sticks we used for asphalt hockey. But a good deal of skill was displayed, and the fun was fast and furious.

The other major day-room sport (at least, judging by the space occupied and the extent to which it encroached on other people's occupations) was table tennis. Again, one of the long and very narrow day-room tables was used, with the benches pushed back. We had standard balls available, and bats of the type then current, the flat plywood covered with thin rubber on one side and sandpaper on the other. The 'net', however, was simply a row of textbooks or novels with the spines uppermost. What with the shape of the tables, and the exaggerated grain of their surface, day-room table tennis was markedly different from any other. There was little delicacy about it, or positional play. It was almost impossible to drop a shot short over the net, and if anyone did achieve it, there was no time to get round in order to return it, when one's normal position was so far back from the net. The most effective game was one of sheer speed, hitting always for the corners, varied by spin if this could be achieved in the split second available. Ten or fifteen minutes of this produced a sweat-soaked shirt and something near exhaustion.

There were all kinds of other activities, covering the whole range from those made compulsory by the authorities, through those which were actively encouraged, those which were tolerated, those which were known about but tactfully ignored, down to those which would certainly have been suppressed if they had been known about. The last-mentioned class was more varied than one might think, even though we were in general a very disciplined and well-behaved school. Perhaps this shows that to be disciplined and well-behaved does not prevent boys from having an extremely lively and satisfying time. It may simply channel enterprise, initiative and even anarchical tendencies into limited areas, where they do not wreck the whole system.

One boy in my house was responsible, if the whispers which went round were reliable, for a whole series of practical jokes. Some of them would certainly have brought serious punishment if the author had been discovered, but he never was, though the whole house, except perhaps the monitors, knew about them. All involved escaping from the locked house at night by means of an underground passage carrying pipes and cables. Some of the tricks were trifling, like removing the works from a gramophone used in class by one of the masters to vary his German lessons. It was of course a clockwork machine (electric record-players were not yet available) and next morning he cranked and cranked away at it without effect. Before a key cricket match against the house which was our greatest rival, to be played on their pitch, he was said to have obscured the whitewashed markings of the wickets at one end, and marked out a fresh one, to make the pitch several yards too long. Another night, he stopped the clock on Big School. This caused considerable chaos, since it was used to govern all our movements, from getting up onwards. The trick we enjoyed most, however, was simple but effective. From the 'tunnel' he got into the same rival house mentioned above, and while they slept upstairs, slippers neatly alongside beds, he mixed up all their shoes in the narrow boot-room downstairs. Their entire house was twenty minutes late for breakfast. In our closely organised routine, it took maybe three minutes for fifty boys to dash into the boot-room, exchange slippers for shoes from one's well-known pigeon-hole, and put the shoes on in the adjoining changing-room. Of course, we could only imagine the scene where every boy, perhaps, found in his pigeon-hole one shoe too big and one too small, but the mental image was delicious. And we did see fifty furious faces, and enjoyed that with discreetly hidden delight.

In his more law-abiding moments, this same boy exercised a considerable talent for caricature. One feat was to produce a sketch of a cricketer in which there was a medley of personal characteristics, a nose here, a particular turn of the wrist there, so that all eleven members of the house cricket team were blended into one. He also did a series of sketches prophesying what various members of the house would look like at the age of forty. I still have copies of two of them. Goldsmith is shown as a well-dressed city gent. He became a banker. I was shown as a portly pawnbroker.

I got involved myself with Timms in activities which were by no means official or universally popular. However, I was merely an unskilled assistant, and I think my participation was never known. He had a passion for explosives, and abstracted small quantities of chemicals from the science laboratories for his private experiments. Several times he made small percussion bombs. He would take one of these up to the top of the house (which itself required a certain daring, as the dormitories were forbidden territory during the day), and toss it out of a window into the middle of a game of asphalt hockey. Before the smoke had blown away, he would have dashed down the back stairs to saunter innocently out and join the argument as to whatever could have happened. Once, too, with me in attendance, he put a charge with a time fuse in the barrel of the old field-gun which stood in the school's grounds as a kind of reminder of the recent war. We were strolling up and down, apparently deep in talk, when it went off with a flash and cloud of smoke, but two small boys were much nearer, and were most agreeably frightened.

However, Timms eventually went too far. He rigged up a small device for producing sulphuretted hydrogen in a passage just outside our dormitory, and started it up as we were preparing for bed. As the gas spread into our community, the rotten-egg smell got stronger. A search was made, the apparatus dismantled, and somehow (I forget how) the culprit was identified. The monitor in charge announced: 'Strictly off the record, I'll give you all two minutes after lights out to deal with him.' When the lights were switched off, there was a wild rush in the darkness. He was not much battered, with everyone getting in each other's way, but he deemed it wise to end his anti-social activities.

I suppose I must make some comment on morals, if only because, thanks to certain writers, people are apt to assume that a boy's boarding-school is necessarily a nursery for homosexual practices. I can say that only once was any kind of advance of this kind made to me, and that came to nothing. One heard talk of some trouble in this house or that once or twice, but as far as my knowledge goes, it was a minor question. As to moral attitudes generally, there was intermittently some nastiness of different kinds, particularly bullying or oppression by a minority of boys, and occasionally oppression by a master. However, I am much more conscious of the broad stream of moral behaviour, of good leadership, unselfish help to the weak and the slow, patience, and courtesy. I visited the school a few years back with two American friends, and as we left we said to each other, 'The boys are so polite.' And a boy still at the school (a rumbustious redhead) told me, 'The masters are very much down on bullying now, even mental bullying. It's almost unknown.'

In the sixty years since I left, I believe that the school has had its ups and downs, in all respects. A school is something like a farm. What you get out of it depends on what you put into it. It needs to be worked, decade after decade, with vigour, skill and determination. It changes and develops. Neglect or misuse damages it, and can even drive it back to the wild. Care and hard work mean rich crops for generation after generation.

It was a surprise to me to find that Christ's Hospital had such long holidays, but this is standard with boarding-schools. With such crowded and active terms, longish breaks must be necessary. We had nearly a month at home each Christmas and Easter, and about six weeks in the summer.

One curious feature was that there was a school rule then that uniform should always be worn in the holidays. There was no way of enforcing this, with the boys scattered all over the kingdom, and I don't suppose there was a single individual who did not, despite the rule, sometimes get into what we called 'townies'. Yet on balance it was usually convenient and advantageous to wear the blue coat and yellow stockings. It was distinctive and dignified, and also you did not have to worry about it. Occasional attention with a clothes brush and the removal of odd grease spots were enough (provided your bands and shoes were clean) to enable you to look smart in any surroundings. In recent years, I have seen senior boys at such events as a charity ball at the Savoy Hotel, when the school was one of the beneficiaries, and at the annual luncheon of the Charles Lamb Society. They always look smart, at ease, and (to repeat a word) distinctive.

When I was at home in the holidays, I took up life with the family very much where it was left off. Naturally, we children were older and bigger each time, and hobbies and occupations changed gradually in accordance with this.

At one time Jimmy and I were much involved with airguns and an air rifle. In our long garden, there was scope for quite elaborate target shooting. One of the most advanced forms was to suspend a small aspirin bottle from the centre of a rustic arch, set it swinging, and try to hit this moving target. A more primitive target was one of the galvanised steel modifying tops on a neighbour's chimney. There were several of these within range, and a hit registered with a pleasing clang. It was, however, wise to attempt these feats from the cover of shrubs, in case an irate neighbour appeared.

We also got involved with explosives. I do not think this had a connection with Timms' activities at school. It arose independently. Jimmy was attracted to chemistry early on, and it eventually became his career. Shortly after he went to secondary school, he acquired with parental permission a stock of chemicals for experiments in the top bedroom, which had become his. He even had a bunsen burner there, and a pensioned-off garden bench to use as a work bench. Here we concocted home-made fireworks which we considered to be superior to the commercial products of the big maker whom we patronisingly called 'Charlie Brock'. From that we went on to make traditional gunpowder. We would go to three separate chemists to buy saltpetre, charcoal and sulphur, which we carefully crushed and blended for various experiments. I think we were equally guarded in what we told our parents as we were with the chemists.

To begin with, we got a large key with a hollow stem from the back door, partly filled it with the blackish powder mixture, added the red tip of a matchstick (not the safety kind with the black tip) and attached to the key with string a large nail which neatly fitted the hollow stem. This was swung by the string against a wall so as to bang the nail into the matchhead and powder, which (with practice) exploded. We also part filled a golden syrup tin with powder, added a slow fuse through a hole in the lid, and buried it a few inches down in a flower-bed. A match to the protruding end of the fuse produced an excellent land-mine effect.

The peak of our achievement, however, was the gun we made from a stair rod. This was a steel tube sheathed in brass. We cut off about fifteen inches of it, and plugged one end with a short piece of steel rod, by heating the tube in the bunsen burner, and letting it shrink on to the plug. This was mounted on a base by some method I do not now remember. A blob of solder near the muzzle made a foresight, and a touch-hole was filed near the plugged end. The projectiles used were ball bearings. The gun was set up on the work bench in the top bedroom, three storeys above the garden, and the target was an old enamel plate set up at the far end of the garden. And we hit it! Several times, as I recall, though not without difficulty.

Ambition, however, has been the end of many technical pioneers from Ikaros onwards. After a time we ran out of ball bearings. Excitement barred us from the time-consuming task of buying more, and we may not have commanded sufficient funds for that, either. As a substitute, we used lead air-gun slugs. The gun got hotter and hotter. One of the slugs, softened by the heat, jammed in the barrel. Impatiently, when we failed to budge it with probes, we decided to blow it out. Jimmy filled the gun to the muzzle with black powder, primed the touch-hole, stood back, and with a paper spill at arm's length touched it off. There was a double 'boom', and the room filled with smoke. Choking, we glimpsed faint flames, tore down the lace curtains which were burning, and stamped them out on the floor. As we did so, we heard racing footsteps on the stairs. We looked at each other's blackened faces. It was Mother, of course.

The first explosion had burst the gun, tattering the steel tube and its brass covering into metallic lace. Remarkably, the only damage besides the curtains was a small hole in the ceiling. But the flash had also set off a pile of magnesium powder to be used for firework making, which was sitting quietly on a newspaper on the end of the bench. Hence, of course, the volume of smoke. Very naturally, this was the end of our explosive experiments.

One Easter holiday turned out quite differently from any other. When I arrived from C.H., I was told that my young brother Don was ill with measles or some similar ailment, and it was thought unwise to expose me, too. It had therefore been arranged for me to spend the holiday with 'Aunt Fan'. My small attaché case was repacked, and (if I remember rightly) I set off at once to walk the half-mile or so to her house.

Miss Frances Chapman was only an honorary aunt. She was actually Mother's cousin. She had managed a shop – her own business, in effect – but had by then, I think, retired, or was about to do so. She lived in a rather good terrace house with a lady companion (Mrs Vincent is the name which bobs up in my mind) and a servant, a bustling little woman of about the same age as the two ladies she looked after. It was an odd setting for a boy of twelve or thirteen, but I quite enjoyed that month with them. They put themselves out to feed me well, and I naturally appreciated that. I can't imagine what I did with myself during the day. Solitary walks and reading, I fancy. But every evening we settled down to a card game, nearly always Bezique with Aunt Fan, while Mrs Vincent sewed. I had never met the game before – at home, it was at first Beat Your Neighbour, later Whist, or Solo with matches for stakes. The quick mathematical estimates of chances in Bezique, and the sudden changes of fortune, fascinated me.

We also played Cribbage, either two- or three-handed, and they showed me Poker Patience. Now, that is a good solo game for odd moments. I must revive my skill at it one of these days.

I suppose the satisfaction of that month came from the quiet undemonstrative affection of the two old ladies, and the utter peace of it all.

Most summers, Dad would scrape together enough money to take us all to the seaside for a couple of weeks. Probably the vast majority of English people with approximately our standard of living did the same in those days. We went by rail, with what seemed to be a mountain of luggage, and there always seemed (to my uncertain memory) to be a standard routine at the departure terminus. At Mother's urging, we would arrive there with all our trunks and packages. (Was there a cat in a basket and a parrot in a cage, or have I borrowed that from cartoons of the period?) Then Dad would stroll off in search of a toilet, and be away for ages. Probably he also had a look at the bookstall, and stocked up with pipe tobacco, too. Meanwhile, Mother got more and more agitated, and we children were stopped from straying by more and more peremptory methods. About the time when the tension was almost unbearable, Dad would reappear, still unhurried. 'Plenty of time', he would say soothingly, and we and our impedimenta would be transferred to platform and train with two minutes to spare.

My wife says I am just the same, except that sometimes I actually cause us to miss the train.

Usually, we stayed at a boarding-house, and at least sometimes we did so on a basis which I believe is not used nowadays. We rented the rooms for a couple of weeks, furnished of course, but we brought our own sheets and pillow-cases, which was one reason for the bulk of our baggage. We also purchased our own food. At least, I remember Mother buying meat and fish, which the landlady cooked for us.

The days were mostly spent on the beach, in the traditional occupations of bathing, paddling, and sand-castle building, but we would also go on country walks, and such things as shrimping among the rocks at low tide. This was, too, the heyday of the concert party. Every little resort had one to entertain visitors nightly on the pier with song and dance, and jokes which we laughed at when the crowd did, whether we understood them or not.

On one holiday at Shanklin in the Isle of Wight, we were thrilled to find we were booked in at the boarding-house where the artistes of the concert party were staying. This was real romance, and we paid our sixpence to see their performances with added excitement at knowing we might also see them at breakfast next day, if they got up early enough. The principals were Wilby Lunn and Connie Hart, a married couple well known on the seaside circuit. In addition, there was the comic, the soubrette, the sentimental baritone, and so on. One only has to re-read J.B. Priestley's *The Good Companions* to bring the group all to life again.

It was at Shanklin, too, I think, that our parents reminisced about an earlier visit, when we had sat on the beach and waved, as the liner *Titanic* went past on her first and tragically final voyage, the wash of her passing sending a rather larger wave up towards our feet. Did I remember seeing the four tall funnels in the haze as she went by a couple of miles off shore? I would only have been five years old in 1912, but I thought I remembered.

In 1920, we made a break with routine. Another of Mother's cousins lent us her flat in Guildford for a month. Dad, in an expansive moment, hired a car and driver to take us down, and in due course bring us back. We were going to be away for so long that at breakfast on the day of departure Mother cleared out from the larder everything which was perishable. It was all set out on the table with the instruction: 'All this has got to be finished up.' I did my best to obey orders, and my last effort before giving up was to put away the last slice of a bread pudding, dark, damp, and rich with dried fruit, spread thickly with the last of a tin of Nestlé's Milk. Strong digestions we had then.

The journey itself was quite an adventure. Had we been in a motor car before? Certainly not for such a long way. The little Surrey villages were half-hidden in the heavy summer leaf of the trees. Our heads were constantly swivelling from side to side, now to see a scarp of the North Downs, now a thatched cottage.

Our destination was in Quarry Street, just off the steep high street. It was the first floor of an old half-timbered house next to the churchyard. The ground floor was a shop, and there was a separate entrance for the first floor, up an alley at the side, facing on the churchyard and its church. Upstairs, the old floors of planks of irregular width sloped sharply in places, and heads had to be ducked under unexpected beams. The windows were low, and one looked through them straight down on to the busy street.

It was a holiday of rich and memorable happiness. What mishaps and difficulties there were do not seriously eclipse all the novel and delightful elements of that month, not even the fact that Don developed mumps. He had to keep in for much of the time, usually with Mother or someone to look after him. It was painful and depressing for him, but for everyone's sakes most of us went out every day and all day.

The two main features of that holiday both had a big effect on us. One was the many days we spent on the river, which was only a few yards away. Dad hired a two- or four-oared skiff, punt or canoe, or more often two in various combinations, depending on what we felt like, and we took with us food enough for the day. The Wey is a small river, and very safe. We fumbled and splashed around, and learned a lot about rowing, paddling and using a punt pole. There was some rain, but also a lot of sunny days, green fields, butterflies, fish and frogs, and everything. It went on long enough to produce a considerable love for what Kenneth Grahame, I think, called 'messing about in boats'. We came back to this many times in the years ahead, and in many places. It may be that this holiday sowed the seed in Jimmy's mind which ultimately drew him into the world of sailing. Dinghy racing, in particular, was a lasting passion with him for many years.

The other feature was the historic places we went to on long country walks. The first, indeed, was reached by the shortest of walks. A few yards along Quarry Street, but on the north side, Castle Hill led up to the major ruin of the town's Norman castle. Guildford, once the capital of a Saxon kingdom, has been an important administrative and trading centre for centuries, so it was natural that the Normans needed a strong fort there. Later on, we visited the ruins of St. Catherine's Nunnery on a bluff overlooking the river, and St Martha's Chapel, on the line of the Pilgrims' Way, where all through the Middle Ages pilgrims had walked and ridden, some from as far west as Winchester, to the tomb of St. Thomas à Becket at Canterbury. One could not help pondering on these links with the past, still so much of the landscape of today.

We walked farther, too, to Compton, and saw the gallery of the painter and sculptor G.F. Watts, and the strange memorial chapel to him, ablaze with mosaics and carved wood. That was a little bit of more recent history, a style in art that was already then out of fashion, though doubtless it would return.

At thirteen, I was very impressionable. When I got back to school, I began to read historical novels and some serious history with enthusiasm, and the following year, when I got a prize (for mathematics), I was lucky enough to receive Conan Doyle's medieval novel *The White Company*. I was not surprised to learn later that Doyle ranked his historical novels far above the Sherlock Holmes stories. I certainly revelled in them in those early 'teen-age' years. To read of an English king like Edward I who spoke no English, and of the devastation in France of the Hundred Years' War, as background to the adventures of the young squire Alleyne Edricson, stirred the blood.

The holidays were really the best parts of my six years at Christ's Hospital. There were other bright patches in term time, but on balance I was miserable more often than I was happy, bored more often than I was interested and excited. Quite a number of the things we were compelled or strongly encouraged to do did not appeal to me in the slightest. The Officers Training Corps doubtless produced some good officers for the armed services. For me it was just 'square-bashing' and route marches in scratchy, ill-fitting khaki, a cap which gave me headaches, puttees which tended to unwind at embarrassing moments, and heavy 'ammunition' boots. Even the routine bouts of shooting at the range brought little pleasure. At first, my eyesight was so bad that I could barely see the box of sand opposite which I lay, and I could only hit the target at twenty-five yards if I pinned the card carefully in the exact centre of the box. Later, it is true, the school got me some better spectacles, in gold wire frames, too, and I got to a fair standard of shooting.

Cross-country running, too, seemed pointless to me, as my black plimsolls thumped deep into the Sussex mud, or slapped along the road edges. I was always towards the end of the pack. I ran because I had to. Perhaps one reason for my poor performance at most sports was that for several years I suffered from that ignominious complaint, flat feet. I had to wear steel supports in my shoes, but ultimately it cured itself.

Sports, therefore, offered no chance for me to win distinction, popularity, or even self-satisfaction. My biggest problem, however, was loneliness. It seems odd that this should be so in a bustling crowd of eight hundred boys, with opportunities for a range of pursuits, some of which would surely give everyone a significant part. Yet I made no close friends. Such friendships as I did achieve were transient and rather shallow. Nothing can sap away so much the natural vigour of a young person, particularly when cut off from the immediate family for most of the year.

No one was to blame except myself. The vast majority of boys thrived. There was no question of my being ostracised or anything, though I think the general opinion about me was pretty condescending.

One incident may throw a little light, and illustrate what I mean. One summer afternoon, I was not required for cricket at my usual level, the house third or fourth eleven, and I drifted up, alone, to watch the school second team play against another school. Our house captain, E.J. Geater, was also captain of the school second. Just before the start, he found that the regular scorer had not appeared, having been taken to the school infirmary with some sudden ailment. He saw me near the pavilion, called me over, and told me to score for our team. This of course was quite an honour, and a contemporary in Mid.B who strolled up was staggered to see me ensconced in the score-box, with the big green book spread out, and pencil ready. I knew fairly well how to keep the score, and the visiting scorer was very expert and helpful in supplying any deficiency in my knowledge of how to record every ball bowled and run made.

After the match, in accordance with custom, the two teams, still in cricketing flannels, went off to six o'clock tea. They would eat on the dais, with maybe two or three masters, before the admiring eyes of the whole school. Geater kindly invited me, as temporary scorer, to join them on the dais, where I would shine in the teams' reflected glory.

I was paralysed with embarrassment. My blue blazer, with the red fleur-de-lis of my house badge on the breast pocket, was old and shabby. At some point I had torn it badly, and one of the maids who cleaned the house had cobbled it together rather roughly. I felt shabby, awkward, clumsy. I mumbled something to Geater, turned hurriedly away, and hid myself in the anonymous clump of juniors at the long house table, with twenty-five boys a side, in the body of the hall.

It would be wrong, though to regard my life in those years as one of 'inspissated gloom'. (Would anyone but Samuel Johnson use such a phrase?) Cheerfulness often broke through. Moreover, I cultivated a stoicism, a resistance to depression, which is no bad thing. By the time I left, I was a solidly built youth, and wore my broadie at a reasonable distance below the waist. I played a just passable game of rugger, and was of course far too big to be bullied. As a Deputy Grecian, I had attained a reasonable intellectual level, and my social standing, as it were, was average. The trouble was that beneath the surface I was still very unsure of myself. I did not really think I had 'made the grade'.

When the day came to leave, I did so with relief, but even then I realised that much had been gained in those six years. That conviction has grown and grown. I feel a real gratitude for it now.

Moreover, I think I overemphasised at the time the negative features of my adolescence, and I have done the same thing in the pages which describe it here. In those years I learnt many of the basic lessons of life. It was a real character-building time. There was a lot of fun and laughter, and of quiet enjoyment of things that interested me, especially books and the green Sussex countryside. Both still bring me deep pleasure. I meet occasionally some of my contemporaries at school. They show no sign that they ever regarded me as the inferior person I thought myself. Indeed, we meet with real warmth and reminisce with carefree laughter. We had some good times together at school, and the difficult parts were valuable too.

10

Cycling. 1923 to 1934

A year before I left school, a new development had begun which had a profound effect on my life. At first, it seemed to be just another hobby, another occupation for the holidays.

Jimmy was at the time rather friendly with a fellow slightly older than him named Harold Greenwood, always called 'Punch' by his friends after the puppet character familiar to everyone. His nose and chin were indeed almost as prominent as those of the puppet. Punch and Jimmy (who by now was at University College, London, and riding there daily on his first bicycle) conceived a plan for a cycling-cum-camping tour in the summer. As we were all inexperienced in these things, they wisely decided to have a trial expedition on a small scale. This was arranged for Easter, 1923, when I was home on holiday, for I was to be allowed to make a third to this enterprise.

To get a clear picture of what followed, it is necessary to dwell on how different conditions were in those days. There was far less traffic on the roads. One tenth as much? Less than that. There were plenty of cars about by the nineteen twenties. They were, however, lighter, slower and with poorer brakes than today. A cyclist could, for example, if he was bold enough, ride a foot behind a motor car, knowing that he had better control than the car did, and that he could pull up quicker. As for speed, it is true that a few years back I was driven along the Kingston By-pass at seventy-five miles an hour in an old open Bentley, but I would think that glorious relic was of the thirties rather than the twenties. We will be nearer the touring speeds of 1923 if I recall a small incident of a very few years later. Out with a couple of friends one evening, we kept pace with a car down a long incline which called for some very brisk pedalling on our part. At the bottom, the driver slowed and pulled in enough for one of us to overtake him, so that he could call out of the window to us, 'You were doing thirty-two down there.'

Besides the cars, there were clumsy motor-coaches, usually called charabancs (pronounced 'sharabangs'), buses (solid-tyred), trams in the cities, and commercial traffic, but there was lots of space in the country, even on main roads. There, too, the tarred surfaces were mostly excellent, on average better than today because they were rarely battered by such heavy vehicles. The side roads, however, were usually untarred. Those most used were smooth enough, but dusty in dry weather and muddy in wet. The less used byways in the country might be potholed, and even grassy in the centre strip.

Bicycles, too, have been hugely improved since then. In fact, we lived through the period of major improvements in the years when I was most active. So in 1923 the generally easier conditions of the roads for cyclists were set off by the weight and clumsiness of most bicycles. Equipment for camping, too, was heavy and crude. If you wanted to buy a waterproof cape for cycling, you would probably go to an 'army disposals' shop selling unused equipment from the recent war, and get an infantryman's cape. This was designed to be used also as a groundsheet to sleep on. It was a rectangle of heavy rubber-coated cloth, with a semicircle cut out of the middle of one side to fit the neck, and buttons for fastening. It was certainly waterproof, but the snag about cycling in it was that the corners of the rectangle hung down in long points, and would catch in the chain or wheel.

Dad, who warmly approved the project, bought a cheap second-hand bicycle somewhere for me. It looked more dashing than the usual 'touring' machine of the day, which had upturned handlebars, a massive frame and wheels, and roller brakes operated by a series of steel rods, but it was an awkward brute to ride. The top tube sloped down from rear to front, giving a very short steering head. The riding position was uncomfortable, and the brakes savage. In front there was a 'pull-up' brake. A short horizontal lever, pulled upwards towards the centre of the handlebars, applied the brake-shoes to the flat part of the wheel's rim. If you put the brake on at all, it was hard to do less than jam it on, and lock the wheel. The hub of the rear wheel contained the drum of a 'back-pedalling brake'. If you took up a free-wheeling position with the pedals at rest, and then put a reverse pressure on the pedals, it did produce a very smooth braking effect. The trouble was that down a long hill it got intensely hot, and it was not unknown for the oil in the wheel bearing to smoke and even catch fire. Still, I was mighty glad to have any bicycle.

A destination for the trial weekend had been agreed, St Neots in Huntingdonshire, some sixty miles away, a considerable distance for novices. It had also been decided that we would not camp, but book accommodation. Jimmy, however, had developed a new notion, on hearing that boats could be hired on the river at St Neots. He wanted to try his hand at sailing. The preparations were simple. Somehow, he got hold of an old bed sheet and three broomsticks. They were to be respectively the mast, gaff and boom. He explained to Mother what he wanted, and she obligingly cut out and sewed a sail to fit the three sticks. When the time came to depart, the spars, with the 'sail' rolled round them, were strapped to the top tube of Jimmy's bicycle.

All went well. The route took us right across London, and up the Great North Road. By the time we reached Baldock we were still lively enough to climb the church tower, and we had the deafening experience of being in the bell-chamber when the clock struck five. Next day, we duly hired a boat. The only one in which the mast could be stepped was a clumsy veteran which had a hole in a thwart forward which had been used for a short towing mast. The hull was thickly tarred, so it was as well that the weather was cool. Jimmy, driven by his daemon, took command and ordered Punch and me to the oars. With some labour we managed to scull the heavy boat a quarter of a mile or so into the teeth of the wind. Then the sail was hoisted, and he took the helm as we majestically sailed back.

Nothing could have been more different from his exploits in later years in the nimble racing dinghies at Cowes, Burnham and elsewhere, when he twice won national championships, but he can still speak with pride as well as amusement of that first sailing voyage.

In due course, the August camping tour was duly accomplished. A tent, blankets, groundsheets, spare clothes and food were somehow lashed on to the bicycles. I was very much the junior member of the party, and I think my load was limited to my few personal possessions and the primus stove. This compact, paraffin-burning gadget was also something widely used by the army in the war, and was a useful means of heating food quickly. It was stowed in pieces in a tin, and was rather heavy. The defect in my case was that the concentrated weight of it just behind the saddle affected the balance of 'me plus bicycle', and even more that of the bicycle by itself, when walking up a hill, for example.

However, that fortnight was a marvellous introduction to some of the joys which became a big feature of the years to come. I can remember the sensual pleasure of hard physical exertion, as well as the dizzy swoop, free-wheeling down the steep hill westward out of Shaftesbury, and the longer, more gradual drift down from the heights of the Mendip Hills. I remember, too, the road threading between the oddly-shaped hillocks of Somerset, past Glastonbury Tor, a landscape full of legends of King Arthur and his knights, and pitching the tent in the orchard of cider-apple trees behind the inn at Sparkford.

There were, too, less pleasant incidents, like waking to a rain-sodden world in a leaking tent, or the moment on a cliff path in North Devon when the bicycle I was wheeling began to heel over, and I feared that it, and possibly I myself, might go over the edge into the rocky sea far below. But these, too, are only parts of the many-coloured picture that remains still fresh in some respects.

Two months before, when I was away at school, there had been another development which was to have a more lasting effect than an individual tour. It was faintly farcical and in some ways unusual, but in the main it was a very ordinary matter. To a limited extent, the development is still continuing more than sixty years later, though much modified. Some would still consider it a humdrum affair, but its persistence is remarkable. There is still, too, a trace of farce about it. In June, Jimmy and others invited a number of friends to a meeting to discuss the formation of a cycling club. It was conceived as being for young men, but so many girls turned up that there could be no question of excluding them. Some of the participants were associated with the Congregational Church which Mother attended, some actively associated, and some less so, as in the case of Jimmy and myself. Curiously, too, a senior member of that church recalled that in 1911 they had had a cycling club for the young men of the church, though the war put an end to it in 1914.

The plan went ahead, with a somewhat mixed group of young people. Many of them were linked by family ties, or school friendships, and so on. They were quite inexperienced as far as cycling went, and everything was highly experimental. The first expeditions were arranged by word of mouth, to places about ten miles away, such as Chessington, Kingston or Richmond. The most convenient time was Saturday afternoon, for those in jobs usually worked in the morning, and tea was arranged at a tea-shop or restaurant. Bicycles were highly miscellaneous, and some of the first ones were barely roadworthy. The men wore tweed knee breeches, or flannel trousers with metal clips at the ankles. The girls wore calf-length skirts with a blouse or jacket, some of them modestly tethering the skirt edge to the shoe with a loop of elastic. But before very long some of the more athletic girls started wearing the 'gym slips' they wore for gymnastics, hockey, or netball, of navy blue serge to the kneecap or just above it, with thick black woollen stockings.

Bit by bit a programme emerged, spreading from the summer months to include occasional and then all winter Saturdays. Runs got longer and to an interesting range of destinations. Clothes became more practical, bicycles better maintained and more suitable for semi-sporting use. The club began to use the network of catering places, cottages, farms, and country pubs, organised by the Cyclists' Touring Club. In the holidays, and more so when I left school, I was caught up in all this. Other people brought their brothers, sisters and friends along.

Our normal procedures in the nineteen twenties would not be possible on today's roads, crowded with fast motor traffic. The police would quickly intervene. Twenty or thirty of us would ride, two by two, as closely as we could maintain position, on the biggest main roads, or narrow country lanes. Assuming that each pair took up an area of road five yards by two, this meant a moving carpet of cyclists half the width of a narrow road, and fifty to seventy-five yards long. It would travel at ten to fifteen miles an hour on the level or downhill. Uphill, this might drop to six. But the motor traffic of that era did not find this too obstructive. Only in towns, and at certain hours, was there much congestion. A car overtaking a cycling club would wait for a straightish piece of road, pull out and accelerate to thirty or forty miles an hour, and overtake the whole group without fuss. Perhaps, on a main road on a bank holiday, it would be difficult. In that case, we might break into two sections, so that drivers could overtake in two jumps, as it were.

We were against riding in single file, thinking that this caused more obstruction. Moreover, it inhibited conversation, which went on almost non-stop, for the roads were so much quieter in those days.

It was the beginning of a boom in cycling, and many clubs were active all over the country. Most of them, although they were often interested in touring, were more or less heavily involved in racing. Moreover, girls were uncommon, except in the various local sections of the Cyclists' Touring Club.

Proper racing, with a simultaneous start, could only be done on a track specially built with steep banking, which usually meant the Herne Hill track in South London. Most racing, however, was done on the road, under restrictions laid down by law. Mass starts were illegal, so all road races were on a time trial basis, each rider starting a minute apart from the next. Races were also supposed not to obtrude on other traffic, so they were mainly started very early on Sunday morning, and the recognised dress was black woollen tights, black jersey and a black alpaca jacket. A strong club would promote an 'open' race, and fields of up to a hundred were common. Around all the big cities, early risers on Sundays would see on the main trunk routes the slender black figures flitting by on their stripped-down machines, silent except for the whirr of tyres and driving chain. The standard distances were twenty-five, fifty and one hundred miles, with longer tests to do the maximum possible in twelve hours or twenty-four hours. An average of twenty miles an hour was known as 'evens'. In the decade or so in which I was actively involved in cycling, it was usual for 'evens' to be beaten over twenty-five miles at the beginning of the period, the course being out-and-home to minimise or average out the wind effects. Then the racing men began beating evens over fifty miles, then a hundred, and eventually over twelve hours, I think. They were even threatening to do so over twenty-four hours as bicycles, road surfaces, and skills all improved.

Our club never took part, as a club, in road or track racing. Some of the lads, however, had a go from time to time under the auspices of one of the racing clubs, such as the Kentish Wheelers or the Norwood Paragon, which they also joined. We, the Streatham Hill Cycling Club, concentrated entirely on touring, on exploring the countryside. As we got more expert, we widened our radius into Southern England, and also prided ourselves on our detailed knowledge. From roads we moved into lanes, then bridle-paths, and even footpaths. The wilder parts were known as 'rough stuff', and carried the additional charm of demanding extra skill from the rider. Often, we deliberately sought out exciting routes, such as the 'cart-track to Buckland', descending the steep southern edge of the North Downs. It was narrow and uneven between the hedges, and cut up into ridges by heavy carts. Most of it was chalk, which rain converted into as slippery a surface as a skating rink. A slight touch on a brake could flick you into an uncontrollable skid, maybe ending in the hedge.

Sometimes the latter part of the outward route would be used for a short competitive purpose, a hill climb to see who was fastest of the more athletic males, a map-reading contest to test mental as well as physical quickness, or a paperchase. The club's first paperchase was, I believe, mounted in the very earliest days of the club, when most of the competitors still crashed about the Surrey lanes and paths on heavy 'upright' bicycles with 28-inch wheels. All honour to them. As we and our bicycles developed in capability, so did the occasional paperchase get longer and more intricate and demanding in terms of terrain. Both sexes participated with abandon in these exercises. On one occasion, at least, both the 'hares' who laid the trail were girls. They reported later that their only difficulty was that one of them could not face laying a trail through a field full of cows. She made a detour while her colleague boldly faced the formidable monsters.

After various trials, we found that the best trail-lying material was confetti. It left clear splashes of multi-colour, if thrown down in handfuls, but wind and rain quickly dispersed it and ensured that the countryside was not permanently defaced. It was too expensive to buy the elegant packets of hearts, crosses and stars which guests sprinkle primly on the bride and bridegroom, but we found a shop which would sell the scrap paper fragments from a confetti factory in twenty-eight pound bags for a small sum. Saddle-bags full of the mixture on the front and back of two bicycles provided a good supply.

One of our paperchases nearly ended in a dead-heat between 'hares' and 'hounds'. I was one of the hares, and as we topped the last ride, the leading hounds sighted us with a chorus of halloos. The only ground left for us to cover was down a steep rough field to the place where we would have tea. Easy! However, our remaining confetti was in the bag behind the saddle of my cycle, a bag which was closed by the usual straps, but also with a lace-up device. I reached behind for a handful of confetti to mark the trail as my partner and I bounced down the hillside, only to get my hand entangled in the lace. In consequence, that last steep hill was done with a precarious one hand for the steering, the wheels bounding over the tufty grass, and the hounds cheering each other on, getting nearer and nearer. We just made it.

All sorts of other mild foolishness might be indulged in after tea, before we set out homewards. Often it would be a walk in the woods or to a hilltop, or impromptu cricket or rounders. Once or twice someone brought out a soccer ball for a kick about, and once even a rugger ball for an even less orthodox match on a sloping field. I can recall some people climbing the jib of an old crane in a deserted quarry, and more than one occasion of sliding on a frozen pond. We even tried to combine two rather idiotic pursuits, cycling on ice and cycle-football, but that was not a success. The trouble was that you could ride in a straight line with a fair degree of control, but if you tried to turn, or to kick the ball, the wheels slid from under you. The girl I was later to marry distinguished herself on one frozen pond by falling hard enough to snap a pedal spindle.

In winter, we would often sit round the fire after tea, talking about every subject under the sun. One particular discussion was as to what date it would be when one returned from flying eastwards round the equator at the same speed as the earth revolved. Supporters were found for at least three different dates, but there was unanimity on one point. When the circumnavigators returned, they would be hungry.

A perennial subject was the design of an ideal bicycle. As cycling clubs generally boomed, a number of 'bespoke' cycle makers developed, who would build bicycles to a customer's specification, as to length of tubes, angle of steering, shape of handlebars, equipment and so on. Grubb, Evans, Selbach, Holdsworth and later Claud Butler were among these well-known names. Many of us patronised them, when we could afford it.

One of my crazier ideas never reached fruition. It was to be a sailing bicycle, and I even got Mr Allin, the Croydon cycle-builder, to agree it would be possible, and to quote me a price. The price was thirty pounds, and I never had that kind of money. In my sketched design, the saddle would be low down over the back wheel, and steering would be by a sort of tiller. She (for a boat is always feminine) would carry a single triangular sail on a steel tube mast, the base of which would sit in roller bearings at one end of the front hub spindle. The lower edge of the sail would be attached by rings like curtain rings to a light boom. An endless cord along the boom (which would be high enough to clear the cycle frame) could be pulled, so that the mast revolved, and the sail instantly furled by rolling it round the mast. I even argued that, just as on water all powered craft had to give way to sail, all motor traffic would have to give way to me as I tacked against the wind up the Kingston By-pass.

Club activities, as the years passed, spilled out further and further into the non-working hours. Saturday afternoons were still the main-stay, all the year round, and in any weather. Some of us, too, would go out all day on Sunday, often down to the south coast, and sometimes right across London to fresh country to the north. A westward run on a day of very dull weather took the club to Stonehenge, and produced the memorable comment from a Yorkshire-born member: 'Fancy cooming all this way to see they moocky grey bricks!' Some used to go out for short rides into the country on weekday evenings. At times, there would be short weekends with a Saturday night at some farm or inn which could feed fifteen or twenty of us, and provide beds, some of them often scattered round the village. In those days, this could be arranged for a few shillings.

Then we began to expand into the longer weekends which were

provided by the Monday 'bank holidays' at Easter, Whitsun and the first weekend in August. The additional bank holidays spawned by different governments since then seem to me to have weakened the impact and the pleasure bank holidays gave in my young days.

The best weekend was Easter. Good Friday at the beginning and Easter Monday at the end meant a four-day break, for few people worked on that Saturday of the year. We found, too, a way of stealing an extra day. By leaving just before midnight on the Thursday and riding all night, we could start our four-day break seventy or eighty miles away from home. Monday had to be reserved for the return trip, but it still left us three full days for exploring country little known to us. A habit grew up, for several years, of spending Easter in the Isle of Wight, and riding down on Thursday night in time to breakfast at Portsmouth or Southampton, to get the first ferry steamer over to the island. It was often very cold during that night ride in early spring, and to avoid carrying extra clothes, the knowing ones would tuck newspapers inside their shirts, and discard them in the morning. They were good insulation.

There were occasional bizarre incidents on these night rides. In those days the roads were not much used at night. In the seventy miles we would meet only dozens of motor vehicles, rather than hundreds. Before the first gleam of light on the horizon, the sleeping birds in the Hampshire woods and hedgerows would somehow get the message from their built-in alarm clocks, and the great dawn chorus would start and quickly swell. Only then would the first glow appear in the darkness behind our left shoulders.

On one of such mornings, in the grey light of dawn, another fellow and I were leading the club's double file down a long slope of the main road towards Southampton. The man on my left was talking to me animatedly, when suddenly, in the middle of a sentence, his voice stopped and he disappeared. My head swivelled to the left, to discover him riding along on top of a roadside bank, some four feet higher than the road. Within a few seconds he came to the end of the bank, his front wheel dipped sharply, and he did a neat nose-dive over the handlebars. (He was – and is – a man who is always neat in everything.) He had gone to sleep. He was quite uninjured, and the only damage to his bicycle was a broken spoke. One of the club who rather specialised in running repairs produced some spare spokes, and fitted a replacement, while the rest of us strolled up and down on the dewy grass. Then on to the breakfast we had booked, marked in memory by a protest from the girls, who were served one egg each with their bacon, against two for the males who, as was pointed out, had ridden no farther than the girls had.

The next stage from long weekends was summer cycling holidays. Most of us had two weeks' summer holiday from work, and through most of that dozen years (and since) parties of two, three or four and occasionally more would set off for a fortnight of freedom. Three factors were standard to all these expeditions. One was the famous 'Bart's' maps, by Bartholomew and Son of Edinburgh on a scale of half-an-inch to the mile, printed in full colour from the luscious green of the valleys to the enticing brown of the high hills. It was always the hills which drew us most. The second was the slim 'C.T.C. book' of the Cyclists' Touring Club, with thousands of addresses for accommodation and meals. And thirdly there was a very modest supply of money. We always reckoned we could tour in Britain at an average cost of ten shillings a day, and get an adequate amount of food into us out of that sum to make the physical effort possible. Even on the low wages of those days, almost any young person could save seven or eight pounds during the year for such a holiday.

As an example, I may take the first tour I did with Con, the girl I later married. Actually, we had had no talk of marriage then, as it appeared an absolute economic impossibility, so why discuss it? However, we were constant companions, and since we were now into our twenties (it was 1930, I think), there was no objection from our respective parents.

We both had good bicycles and had fitted the back wheels with a fixed cog on one side, for good control on the slower surfaces, and a free-wheel on the other, for the more mountainous areas. We wore shirts and shorts of khaki drill, with a light jacket. A minimum of spare clothes and nightwear, tools and maps, was carried in bags behind the saddle, with proper light oilskin capes designed by a cyclist for cyclists. Also, to save weight, we had sent spare shirts and socks on to await us at one or two post offices at strategic points, and we would then post the soiled things home.

The route was up the eastern side of England. We did ninety-eight miles the first day, then on through Lincoln, Doncaster, and laterally across the Yorkshire Dales. We crossed into Scotland at Castle Bar to Melrose, Selkirk and then westwards. Along by St Mary's Loch, the headwind was so cold that Con retired into a convenient group of trees, and put her pyjama jacket on under her shirt. We re-entered England near Carlisle, did a quick tour of the Lake District, mostly in torrential rain, and continued through Lancashire and Derbyshire, including some 'rough stuff' in Dovedale. The last night we stayed in Stratford-on-Avon, and on the final day we did about a hundred miles, getting home in time for a late tea. We had covered some eight hundred and forty miles in sixteen days, mostly in hill country.

It may be worth recording how the girls progressed, stage by stage, from wearing calf-length skirts to shorts. It was directly connected with the growing determination of most of the club to be all-weather cyclists. If this was to be, rain-soaked skirts clinging to the lower limbs were clearly unbearable. Gym slips were not really the answer. One of our girls, aged twenty-odd, travelling by tram to pick up her bicycle from the repairer before going out with the club, was given by the tram conductor, after one glance, a half-price ticket for a child under fourteen. It was amusing, but hardly dignified.

My wife-to-be, Constance, always called 'Con' in the club, heard that the wife of a well-known racing cyclist turned cycle-builder named W.F. Holdsworth, had developed a special outfit for the girls called a 'rational costume'. She went to investigate, and ordered a suit in a heather-mixture tweed. It was certainly very elegant, a full-skirted knee-length jacket over narrow-cut knee breeches. These were loose over the knee, and buckled below the knee, very comfortable to wear – with one exception. On a wet and windy day the knees quickly got sodden. So, after a while, she cut off the knees. Within months, most of the club girls were in shorts.

H.W. 'Bunny' Austin, the tennis player who was the first man to wear shorts at the Wimbledon tournament, was very amused by this story. It was roughly contemporaneous with his own move for freedom and comfort. In *A Mixed Double*, the joint autobiography he wrote with his actress wife Phyllis Konstam, he tells how he was leaving his hotel with an overcoat over his shorts, when a young hotel porter said, 'Excuse me, Mr Austin. I think you've forgotten your trousers.'

In successive summer holidays I toured in every English county except Norfolk, in much of Scotland, and the borders of Wales. Others of us ventured overseas, drawn as ever to the hills and mountains, where the long climbs, often walked, were considered well worthwhile for the bold vistas and exhilarating downhill swoops they made possible. They went to the Black Forest in Germany, to Norway, the Pyrenees, the Alps and the Dolomites.

One other activity might be mentioned, which really developed out of our enthusiasm for 'rough stuff'. I am not sure that we originated cross-country cycle racing, now called 'cyclo-cross' and an international sport, but we were certainly in at the very beginnings of it. As an extension of our paperchases and such, we instituted a club cross-country championship. It was run as a time-trial, the competitors starting at minute intervals. The course was twelve miles of the roughest country we could find, so rough that even the best riders took something like an hour to cover it. Mostly, we found that the machines we used for general club riding were suitable, though some of us fitted lower gear ratios. The one customary modification was to remove the mudguards, to prevent the heavy winter mud from clogging the wheels. It naturally meant getting pretty filthy.

At about the same time a well-known club in South London, the Centaur Bicycle Club, decided to promote an invitation cross-country team race. The main aim, I think, was to liven up the winter off-season, for road racing was mainly confined to the summer months. Many famous clubs were invited, and we were included, on the strength of our known interest in mudlarking. The course was very similar to that used in our club championship, and in the same area, including parts of Headley Heath. (The National Trust now owns it, and cycling is banned.) There was a prize for the fastest individual, but the main interest was in the team results. Each team was of four riders, and the third fastest in the team counted. This allowed for one to crash or tire, and encouraged the fastest in the team to help the others. The competition was run for several successive years, and in the last year forty-four teams were entered, a total of one hundred and seventy-six riders.

My memory is fairly sure that we put in two teams the first year, and came first and second. In the following years, we usually took two of the first three team prizes. I was not a star performer, but I still have in a cupboard a silver medal and a bronze.

One particular race is very vivid in certain respects, including the very narrow margin by which we gained our place. Teams were despatched at minute intervals. I was teamed with two brothers, Jack and Fred Richardson, and Raymond Stevens, always called 'Inky' – Stephens' ink was very widely advertised then. It was a clear bright Sunday morning, with little wind, but there had been frost in the night. In the shadowed lanes and bridle-paths the mud was mostly hard and uneven, but where the sun had shone for a few hours on the open heath, the ice in the ruts was melting, and in unpredictable places there were patches of greasy mud. It soon became clear that skill rather than brute force might decide the day. We were probably not so powerful as the racing men who made up much of the field, but our extensive experience of rough ground was extra important on such a day. Skids were common, and those who fell off least often might win.

The Richardsons set a hot pace, and maybe halfway through Inky began to fade. We all, including him, agreed to leave him to follow, and press on. All three of us felt strong, and took turns in leading. However, I had one skid too many. The track over the heath dipped into a hollow where the sun did not reach. As we plunged into it, flat out, my front wheel found the edge of a frozen rut, and before I could think I shot over the handlebars, landing on my head on icy ground. Of course, I rolled on impact, and I had thick hair which cushioned it a little. I got up dizzily, grabbed the undamaged bicycle, and threw myself at the pedals to catch up the other two, who were looking back anxiously. Then we were away again.

At the finish, we were going great guns. There was a short piece of road before the tape, which had been set up near the pond at Walton-on-the-Hill. A fair crowd was awaiting us. Somehow, in those last seconds, we decided on a grand-stand finish, and adjusted our speeds to get in line abreast. Then we went hell-for-leather for the line. The spectators drew back. At the very last moment, a small white dog, barking merrily, ran out. One of the Richardsons missed him by feet. I was in the middle of the three, and had no chance. My front wheel hit him in the ribs, and I actually crossed the finishing line in mid-air. I clearly remember gripping the handlebar in the hope of straightening out so that I landed with the wheels parallel to the line of flight, but I failed to do so. The front wheel crumpled to one side, and I finished untidily and bloody on the gravel. Later, we jumped on the rim of the wheel until it was in sufficient shape to ride home. The dog was not seen again. But we got our four medals.

Another year, one of the cinema newsreel companies sent a team to film 'the Centaur cross-country'. They found it extremely funny, especially where the course took us down a muddy slope which was actually too steep to ride down. There were three methods of tackling this. You could try to ride down, and fall off; you could dismount and run down it with the bicycle, ending in a welter of wheels and legs; or you could throw the bicycle down the slope, and slide down after it. The following week we all went to the cinema, not for the feature film, but to see the Universal News. We had to admit it was funny. I glimpsed myself at one point. My career as a film star lasted one second.

Have I given the impression that we were a bunch of half-wits playing the fool in a variety of silly ways? If so, the picture still needs to be filled out somewhat.

The most conspicuous feature of those years with the club was perhaps our general attitude to life. We cultivated equanimity and a positive attitude to whatever happened, not as a deliberate policy or anything like that, but because this produced the kind of social atmosphere we liked.

It was, for example, not considered right to be ruffled if a motorist drove too close, if a policeman was officious, or a caterer grasping. Politeness was the rule, possibly tempered with humour afterwards, as when someone was charged with riding without a light. The same applied within the club. Occasionally someone would join in our activities, and prove to be out of tune with the general attitudes. He might be arrogant, use bad language, drink more than a modest amount, or something like that. He rarely got as far as applying for membership, for he simply felt unwelcome.

Coping with the weather also had a lot of effect on our attitudes. If a group of people ride ten miles in company in a dense fog, they have to exercise quite a little self-restraint. The same can apply to extremes of heat, cold and wet. I once met Sir Ranulf Fiennes, the explorer who led the Transglobe Expedition to the South and North Poles. He said that in selecting personnel to operate in conditions which were extreme in every way, they applied one criterion only. Could they get on with other people? If so, it was easy enough for people to learn radio-communications, navigation, or engine maintenance (at forty degrees below zero). If they could not work as a team under strain, technical skills were useless.

On one of our Saturday runs, I was riding with Sam Watts, an unusual character with a philosophical turn of mind. It was a day of torrential rain. It forced its way in through the collars of our capes to make icy rivulets inside our shirts. Our shoes were full of water and squelched at every pedal stroke. Each car which passed sent a wave of spray across our legs. We were discussing the 'back to nature' movement, the Woodland Folk and other groups who talked a lot about the simple life and getting in tune with the elements. Sam and I both felt this was rather self-conscious and a trifle overdone. Then he said, 'Well, I suppose you could say that's what we're doing at this moment – getting in tune with the elements.' And he started chanting quietly to a popular tune of the day, 'Oh, we're in tune with the el-e-ments, and they're in tune with us.'

One Christmas-time, a score or so of us had arranged to spend Boxing Day at a favourite place of call, the Volunteer Inn at Sutton Abinger on Leith Hill, some twenty-five miles out. Harry Stephens the licensee, a delightful old countryman, had promised us a turkey midday dinner with all the trimmings. It turned out to be that rarity in southern England, a white Christmas, with lots of snow. We duly assembled at the appointed meeting place, and set off. On the main roads, where the traffic had churned up the snow, it was possible to pick one's way without too much difficulty. On the side roads, things got worse and worse. Some two or three miles from our destination, the last lane was blocked with drifts four feet deep. We stacked the bicycles in a shed, and continued on foot. For part of the way, we walked on top of the wayside hedge, which gave a firmer footing than the furrowed field. To help us along (you never knew what would happen out with the club) Freddie Richardson produced a piccolo from an inside pocket, and played marching tunes.

Harry Stephens was amazed to see us. He had never imagined we would make it. Nothing could be done about lunch then, but he offered to serve it four hours later, and meanwhile to give us our usual substantial tea. As soon as this was on the table, he went out in the garden to dig out Brussels sprouts from under two feet of snow. Darts and other amusements passed a pleasant afternoon, and we went back as we came, though of course in darkness, which slightly increased the hazards.

Years later, I called in at the Volunteer. The group photograph which Jack Richardson took of us outside the inn in the snow was still in pride of place in the bar.

'The knock' was another hazard with which we learnt to cope. It also had other names, like 'acid' and 'taking a packet'. Maybe it is the cyclist's equivalent to 'the wall', which marathon runners talk about. At some time, well along on a long ride, one's legs seem to lose all power, probably the back aches, and all one wants to do is to go somewhere and die. Sometimes it is associated with hunger (when it's 'the hunger knock'), and this may bring stomach pains too. A little easily digestible food may help, and hot tea usually will cure it, but these are not always available when most needed. So how do you cope? Are you prepared to go on when you feel like death, and on, and still on? Will your pride allow you to accept the pressure of a friendly flat hand between the shoulder blades to help you up the hills, and not hold back the group?

Another testing point is the failings of others, especially of one's friends. Can you not only bear with these failings, but actually find amusement in them? Midge, a red-headed girl in the club, was not really a problem. Her good nature made her generally popular, but crises often surrounded her. Efficient brakes were essential for a group of people riding in close formation, but somehow her brakes seemed to fail quite often. On one long and steepish hill, we heard a high-pitched cry of 'Can't stop! Can't stop!' from the back of the column, and Midge shot through the entire club from end to end, missing everyone by inches. I think she was stopped in the end by someone grabbing her skirt, and braking enough for two. Another time she got involved with a herd of cows crossing the road, emerging from the mêlée with a tuft of coarse hair wedged in the lever of her bicycle bell. Such incidents may be funny, but when repeated are quite disruptive.

Then there was Bob, the Frenchman who came on a club weekend, his one and only appearance with us. He was willing enough, but completely inexperienced, and the machine he rode (doubtless borrowed from a friend of a friend of the club member who misguidedly brought him) was an old rattletrap with various mechanical faults, and a very perished inner tube on one wheel. This kept on puncturing, always in the depths of the country, far away from any possible cycle shop. We mended twelve holes in it at twelve different points of that two-day trip, and all remained cheerful. I'm not sure that Bob (who spoke almost no English) even noticed that proceedings were a little out of the ordinary.

Relationships between the sexes were also somewhat unusual, though newcomers to the club normally dropped into the pattern so quickly that it might suggest that our ways were the normal ones, and others were abnormal. The girls demanded no privileges and, so far as the differences in physical strength allowed, did everything that the boys did. On the longer runs, perhaps, fewer girls would appear, but some of them would peel off a hundred miles or more in the day as often as anyone. They also took part in the embroideries to our activities, like heaving bicycles over padlocked gates, or crossing a brook by riding across a single-plank bridge. Some at least objected to being helped, so we males had to use tact in such things as adjusting the pace to their needs, mending their punctured tyres, and such. Above all, the code we imposed on ourselves avoided any embarrassment to the girls by word or action. Even where a couple were engaged, or firmly attached in that direction, they avoided open evidence of affection, for the whole crowd was regarded as one unit, and everyone needed to be considered, liked, and if necessary cared for. Chivalry is not too strong a word to describe the attitude which was never referred to, but was cultivated whenever we were together.

The atmosphere was remarkably free of sexual overtones. The girls never dressed or behaved provocatively. Some of us had been rather strictly brought up, and with many sisters and brothers mixed in the group, there were natural checks against anything loose or improper. Yet we were entirely relaxed, free and informal.

We were not paragons, of course. We had all the faults everyone has. But to preserve our way of life we had to maintain certain standards, and this we almost always contrived to do.

In doing this we built up a corporate spirit which still persists to this day. The last reunion I went to brought together fifty-five people, including some wives, husbands and children. In fact, the club itself remains in being, despite the vast social changes in the past sixty years. A few continue to cycle for pleasure, both some who joined after my time, and some contemporaries of mine. One group of four of these, between seventy-five and eighty years old, meet occasionally for rides in the country, sometimes in areas little changed since their youth. They self-mockingly call themselves 'the geriatric section'.

There are still close links between many of these old friends, though some live now in Australia and the U.S.A. When we meet, the old adventures are recalled, and the old jokes are made over again. Something worthwhile was developed in us in those years. A number of us, perhaps a disproportionately large number, have had quite distinguished careers. Many stable marriages began as club friendships. These values cannot be measured quantitatively, but there is no doubt that they exist. We were a mixed bunch, from various social backgrounds and levels of income, but all acknowledge having drawn out more from our associating together than we individually put in. What was it? About the only thing we would all admit to would be the 'club jokes', the slightly zany humour, often only intelligible to ourselves, which provided a distinctive tang to our doings. (So we thought. But I once heard something very like it between strangers to us, taking tea at the same cottage as us. One said to the other, 'And none of your mouchoir-pouchoir.') A lot of it came from a play on words, like the puns for which Charles Lamb the essayist was so well-known amongst his friends, Coleridge and Wordsworth, Dyer, Manning, and Haydon the painter. But the puns with which Lamb covered his stammer, and over which his friends chuckled, were only the outward sign of a rich and many-sided group of relationships. In a way, it was the same with us.

11

Boys

Although cycling filled so much of my non-working hours in those years, it did not exclude some other activities. For example, there was a period when I helped, one evening a week, at a boys' club in the New Kent Road, one of the poorest areas of London. The thing I remember clearest about that is teaching the boys boxing. I knew little about it, but a lot more than they did. They were a fairly wild lot. Once, a boy invited me to put on the gloves with him. There was something in his look which made me a bit suspicious, but I agreed. As soon as we squared up to each other, three other boys attacked me from the rear. It seemed to be the plan that they would hold me while the boy with the gloves pummelled me. Their average age was about thirteen, so that there was a sort of sportmanship in it. I felt that the issue had to be resolved quickly, so I swung my shoulders violently, to throw off the boy on my back with his arms round my neck, shook off the two who were clinging to my legs, and hit the boy with the gloves hard enough on the chest to knock him across the room. Then I said, 'One at a time! You can all have a turn later.' This seemed to appeal to them. The boy with the gloves got up, and we boxed three one-minute rounds in the most gentlemanly manner. The others duly had their turns, too. No wonder I enjoyed my evenings with them.

Some years later, I got involved with boys in a more organised way. There was a Boy Scouts group attached to the church to which the cycling club was (very nominally) also attached. It had the usual three sections: Wolf Cubs for the smallest boys, Scouts up to fifteen or sixteen, and Rover Scouts for the youths and young men. The highly competent scoutmaster in charge of the middle group, and in overall charge of the whole lot, had decided to give up for reasons of health, and an urgent word went round that a successor was needed, fast. No one could be found to take it on. The assistant scoutmaster and one or

112

two of the Rovers belonged to the cycling club, so I heard all about it.

I cannot say just why I raised the possibility of my becoming the scoutmaster of the 12th Streatham troop. I had never had anything to do with the Scout movement. I suppose it must have been sympathy for people who needed help, and a vague inclination towards public service of some kind. After all, I did what I wanted to do for so much of my time that maybe something was needed to balance that attitude a bit. My tentative enquiry as to whether I might be able to help was taken up with enthusiasm. All doubts were swept aside.

The main problem was my utter inexperience. The headquarters of the movement kept some supervision over the thousands of separate groups by providing that their leaders (usually called scouters) were reasonably qualified to look after a group of boys. A scouter had to have been a Scout to obtain a warrant from headquarters, and even then he could not take boys to camp unless he had a camping certificate. The result was that a few weeks later, when a dozen or so Scouts of the 12th went off to summer camp under their old leadership, the party included a very large 'tenderfoot' wearing his first Scout uniform, but without the most elementary of rank and proficiency badges. I had to learn my knots, the use of a compass (I did know that), and other simple tests for small boys. Still, they were an agreeable bunch, and keen to make me feel at home.

This must have been about 1931, so I must have been about twenty-four years old. The externals of scouting have changed immensely since then, so it may be worth recording some of the details of a camp in that period. Short trousers were of course no novelty to me. The broad-brimmed hat was, but I found it valuable in hot sun, or in penetrating thick wet woods, which perhaps was a more frequent experience than the hot sun in English weather. I think we took my bicycle and one other to camp with us, to help with communications, and with shopping if we ran short of food, but mostly we moved on our feet, either walking or at 'scouts' pace', which was twenty paces at a walk, then twenty at a trot. Tents (which were heavy, since they included at least one ex-army bell tent) and other impedimenta, were carried on a trek-cart. This vehicle, of wood and iron, with a shaft and handles for pulling and iron-tyred wooden wheels, was a safe and sure, if slow, means of transport. Usually, two of us pulled and two or more pushed.

The day before we left, the heavy stuff was taken to the terminus at Waterloo by a trek-cart party, a journey of three or four miles on main roads, bumping over the tramlines here and there. The cart was then dismantled to its base and axle, wheels, sides, and shaft, and everything was deposited at the left luggage office overnight. When we all met at the station next day, we recovered all the stuff, and assembled and loaded the cart to run it on to the platform to the guard's van of the train, where it was all dismantled again and stowed aboard. On arrival (at Brockenhurst in the New Forest that year) the cart had to be reassembled on the station platform, loaded, and pulled a mile or two to the camp site over rough country, including fording a stream or two. Most modern boys would find such a journey absurdly laborious in this motorised age.

Camp was full of procedures and experiences strange to me. I will only mention one or two of them, the rope we rigged in a big oak-tree, so that we could swing Tarzan-fashion across a deep stream – beginners nearly always grasped it too low, and swung through the water with a chilling splash; the dead thorn-tree we dragged bodily, roots and all, out of a swamp to burn on our camp-fire; and the adder which was found to be living near our flagpole – it was quiet and peaceable, so we all handled it, and I saw its forked tongue exploring the short sun-bleached hairs on my forearm.

It will be gathered that the 12th Streatham Scouts were inclined towards originality, even eccentricity. I discovered this early on, when I found that it was customary to test whether a boy had actually learnt to tie a bowline, by having him tie the knot round his own chest with a light rope. He was then lowered from the gallery of the church hall where we met each week. If the knot gave way, he would of course have failed the test. It was even said that in past years, when the group was without a scoutmaster and was therefore officially de-registered by the Boy Scouts Association, the senior boys continued to run a programme, and even to organise summer camps. I am sure that the disapproval of the authorities would have been tinged with a certain admiration of the enterprise involved.

Scout troops, I found, varied a great deal in character. At one end of the scale, there were ultra-smart uniforms, precise drill on parade, and a bugle band. At the other, there was a highly informal attitude, with a lot of woodcraft and knock-about activity. We were well into the latter end of the scale. It was said that of our two dozen young roughs, half were children from the big block of police married quarters nearby, and the other half from families which, as it were, supplied the police with most of their work. It was a libel, of course, but it had a little truth in it. The policemen's sons were as tough as old boots, and could be very unruly, too. Some of the others came from the poorest streets. One mother successfully begged us, with a contribution of sixpence towards the cost, to take her boy to camp, though his entire equipment for a week comprised the shirt, shorts and broken plimsolls he was wearing. He ultimately got together a uniform of sorts from items discarded as worn-out by his fellow Scouts, and wore it with pride.

However, the mixture was actually very varied. I can still picture clearly various unusual boys, young Vaucher, the neat precise son of a Swiss watchmaker; Ray Goby, small and almost too good-looking but mad on our rougher games, who fought in the war in a tank regiment and became an insurance broker at Lloyd's; Archie Drage, dark, compact and athletic, who became a fireman, then went to Australia to be a farmer, and ended up organising a volunteer fire brigade in a bush township in New South Wales.

We had good times together, mixing training and camping with all sorts of games, indoor and outdoor, usually very physical, sometimes invented by ourselves. We played single-sticks, which must, I suppose, have been played by English boys since the days when each man carried a sword. But has anyone but us attempted single-stick bouts on bicycles, indoors? Grazes were common, with our knees and forearms bare, but no one was seriously hurt.

I had three years as a scoutmaster. Then it became clear that increasing activities in other fields meant I could not give the troop the time it required, so I resigned. Yet it had engaged my heart and loyalty so much that I was constrained to keep some connection as a Rover Scout (they now call them Venture Scouts) for several years more. The thing which drew me so strongly was not the activities, the organisation, or even the people involved. It was the inner spirit of Scouting, a thing rarely talked about, except on such formal occasions as the induction of new members, or for a brief moment or two just before a parade was dismissed. Scouts could be of any religion or none, but were expected to practise their religion if they had one. They were, too, called to a general loyalty to God and their country. The Scout Law set up ten qualities as characteristic of what a Scout should be. 'Brotherly, courteous, kind' was one line in the catalogue.

At the time, I had no concrete code myself. To me, God was something some people believed in, but of whose very existence I was profoundly sceptical. My tendency was to sneer at it. The Scout Law, however, seemed to make sense. The ten points made a clear code which could be a basis for decision-making. So I slurred over what I thought of as the God issue, and concentrated on this moral core of things. I don't recall that I ever talked this over with anyone. Probably I was too shy, prickly, and conscious of inadequacy to do so. The lead I was supposed to give the boys on these matters was also slurred over somewhat. I concentrated on the outward things, the physical activities and so on.

Sometimes, of course, the basic issues would break through. We had a monthly church parade, but this implied little. Mainly, I saw that the boys were clean and orderly, and let my mind wander during the sermon. However, I do recall a weekend camp I ran, one of several for patrol leaders, the non-commissioned officers, as it were, the most responsible boys of the whole Streatham district. It was mainly concerned with camping skills, but the boys had to be given time, if they wished, to attend church on the Sunday morning. One of the boys was a Catholic. He very much wanted to go to Mass, but could not face going by himself to a strange church. So I went with him. The service in the crowded village church (mostly in Latin) obviously meant much to him, and indeed to the whole congregation. It meant nothing to me, but I could not forget that devout mass of people. What was it that I was missing?

It happened, too, that Scouting brought me brief touches with wider events. Twice in those few years I was at major rallies when the founder of the movement, Lord Baden-Powell, was present. It was not so common to see him, when the membership had swelled into millions, spread over most of the world. On both occasions the weather was horrid, with torrential rain. It was alleged that this always happened when the Chief Scout was there, so 'Chief's weather' was accepted as traditional. He was a great age then, and ambled round the tents and displays on the saddle of a placid horse. But there he was.

Later, one of my last Rover Scout activities was at the coronation of King George VI in 1936. The Duke of Norfolk as Earl Marshal was in charge of the ceremonies, supported by the police. They asked for and obtained auxiliary help in traffic control at Westminster Abbey from a hundred and twenty Rover Scouts, and I was asked to lead a party of eight from Streatham. We were on duty from 5.30 a.m. for seventeen hours, with just an hour's break for lunch during the service in the Abbey. The main task was to keep moving the three thousand cars which delivered and collected the guests, most of the time in pouring rain. The bonuses were a point-blank view of the King arriving in his red velvet 'cap of maintenance' (worn by the monarch only on this occasion before his crowning) with the Queen and the two little princesses, and quite a few glimpses of notable people. An air marshal, alighting from a limousine in full dress uniform, wedged a packet of sandwiches into his plumed helmet, before settling the helmet on his bent arm and marching into the Abbey. I heard a Cabinet minister I recognised from the Press suggesting to a friend after the ceremony that they could get 'quite a decent lunch' in the House of Lords; and I even had a short conversation myself with the German ambassador, Herr von Ribbentrop.

There is one other matter which might be mentioned here, although it is not related to my touches with the boys' club and the Scout movement. The early thirties were also the period of a very active peace movement, and at one point I joined the Peace Pledge Union. This meant a pledge never to use or countenance the use of weapons of war, a decision so sweeping as to make the aims of today's Campaign for Nuclear Disarmament look rather milk-and-water-ish. Obviously, one could only make such a pledge under a powerful urge of altruism. In the following year or two, the increasing menace to other countries of Fascism in Italy and National Socialism in Germany gradually convinced me that there could be some things worse than war, some situations where to fight could be a lesser evil than submission. I therefore sent in my resignation from the PPU, explaining this.

It so happened that twenty-five years later I began a protracted, if somewhat tenuous, personal link with the North Atlantic Treaty Organisation, as a technical adviser to one of their civilian committees. This strongly reinforced the amended view I formed back in the thirties, and it was particularly interesting to get a glimpse of things from the inside. I have yet to hear the slightest word of an aggressive nature from anyone connected with NATO. The body has been in existence for the best part of half a century now, and it has yet to move a single fighting man into an adversary's territory. Yet its provision for arms and its preparation for fighting are developed further each year.

Many, perhaps most, people are convinced that NATO's preparedness for war has actually prevented war in Western Europe a number of times already. Certainly, it is not the weapons which make war. It is the people who control them who do that. One might consider Switzerland, which has had universal military service for many years. Every eligible Swiss has his uniform and rifle at home, and has regular training. A banker friend of mine spent the whole winter of 1939/40 above the snow-line with the Alpine troops, and a

British general told me that at that time the Swiss army had more anti-tank guns than the British and French armies put together. It was no wonder that the country was kept safe from invasion – General Guisan, who was in command, became a national hero without firing a shot. And no one would think of describing the well-armed Swiss as warmongers.

I do not regret my brief essay into pacifism. When a young relative told me (with a trace of belligerence in his attitude) that he had joined and supported CND, I was able to tell him that at about his age I had been of a similar opinion, perhaps more extreme, though I had had second thoughts later. And I could also say with sincerity that I thought it far better for him to believe in something, whether he was right or wrong, than to believe in nothing.

12

Girls

When I sat on a jury in London's Central Criminal Court at the Old Bailey, I heard witness after witness, hand on testament, swear to tell 'the truth, the whole truth and nothing but the truth'. I will certainly not do that in this chapter. The truth will be aimed at, and also nothing but the truth, but I see no virtue in telling the whole truth on such a subject. So I must see how I can give an honest picture, without allowing certain necessary omissions to be misleading.

What should be the aim of writing this chapter? Not, I think, the revealing of secrets. Not a catalogue of events. Not as a record of the maturing of certain powers, which have been pictured by poets, novelists and biographers countless times, and in an equal variety of ways. The angle which I hope to picture, to fit in with the general pattern of this book so far, is that of what forces affected the development of the story I am trying to tell.

Six years at boarding-school had all but insulated me from girls, except for fleeting, superficial contacts during the holidays. When I was let loose into society generally, my natural encounters with the other sex were quite limited. When I began work, there was just one woman in my office with the men and boys. In the cycling club, as I have explained, there was a somewhat formal and arm's-length relationship between the sexes. These circumstances, added to my natural awkwardness (and even my status as a younger brother) all helped to make me a slow starter and late developer where girls were involved.

I did find myself included in quite a flow (though hardly a flood) of social events, to a large degree with the same crowd of people, mostly slightly older than me in those first years. Parties were often given in homes for birthdays and such, with round games, singing round a piano or occasionally more formal solos, and dancing. In our particular crowd, parties were lively, fairly noisy, but pretty decorous. The cycling club occasionally organised a dance, hiring a hall and a semi-professional band. So did many other clubs and organisations, so that sometimes we would be all friends together, and sometimes a few of us would be in a group amongst a crowd of strangers.

Looking back now, I can see how much these affairs were coloured in my mind and feelings by those extraordinary and mysterious beings, girls. They really did seem very strange to me. I suppose they still are. Women's mental processes, reactions and attitudes are still in most respects beyond my comprehension.

However, even at a distance I could be deeply stirred by the slightest incident, or even by a notion. No doubt this was all part of the process of growing up, physical and chemical, as well as emotional.

There was the incident involving the girl I will call E. Nothing could have been more trivial, I suppose. It was at one of those birthday parties, lots of brothers, sisters and cousins as well as school friends, and we played several childish games, suitable for people half our age. One of them (could it have been Postman's Knock?) involved calling a member of the opposite sex out of the room for a few moments, and E. called me out. She was rather a beauty, plumpish, and with rich dark eyes and hair. The normal thing in the game was a playful peck of a kiss, or thereabouts, but when the door shut on us, E. threw her arms round me, pressed herself against me, and gave me a kiss which in a Hollywood film would have been prolonged enough to bother the film censors. Then with a mischievous grin she shot off.

I don't know how long that incident haunted me. It left me breathless and dazed at the time (I was still in my teens). I used to lie awake thinking about it, and wondering when there would be a chance for more of the same. But there never was. On the rare occasions when I met E., she was pleasant, but offhand. It had just been a momentary joke. But I cannot begin to describe the stirrings in my blood, the imaginings, the utterly foolish dreams that flowed from it.

Then there was V., a girl very much on the fringe of our circle. She had some pretensions to style – big grey eyes, long dark lashes. I believe she had a French mother. I forget how I managed to engage her interest, but we did meet from time to time, at her house, and talked at length. Mostly, I think, it was about books, and she introduced me to several authors. One of them was Jeffery Farnol, whom I then found romantic and exciting, though I now find him unreadable. Now I come to think of it, one of his titles was *The*

Amateur Gentleman, a Regency story about a man who tried to be something he was not. Was V. trying to say something particular to me in recommending it? She was a fine dancer, and I think we once went to a dance together.

Then, one day, I was supposed to be calling for her (or was it just calling on her?) and I arrived ten minutes after the appointed time. The house was dark, and no one answered the bell. I waited in growing embarrassment, and eventually left. I called unannounced on another day. She said she did not wish to see me, and closed the door.

M. was a very different sort of girl, not at all outstanding as regards looks, fair and with little bright eyes, which were always merry, and which almost disappeared when her face crinkled up in a laugh. For a fancy-dress party she borrowed my small brother's Christ's Hospital uniform. In the long blue coat, black breeches, and yellow stockings and her hair stuck down with brilliantine, she looked like a boy – except that no boy ever had a grin like that. She also was a fine dancer, and I went to several dances with her. I was decidedly below average as a dancer, but with her I always enjoyed it, and almost felt expert. Of course, at times I felt sentimental towards her, and can still visualise an occasion at her garden gate after midnight in the moonlight. But she was engaged to a young man working overseas. She was devoted to him, and to me she was wholly friendly, but also completely proper. So we could have much fun together, without ever engaging strong feelings.

I promised there would be no catalogue, so I will move on at once to the one relationship which persisted all through this period, slowly but strongly developing, which mattered more than any other, and which is, I think, still developing. At least, I hope it is.

When I first knew her, she was almost a wisp of a girl, five feet two inches tall, and weighing about seven stone – ninety-eight pounds. To childhood friends Connie, and to the cycling club known as Con, she now prefers her proper name Constance. Her looks were not striking, her colouring pale, but she moved springily, almost with dash, slender, upright and trim. She was quite a good gymnast and played various games, including cricket. It was in the cycling club that I really got to know her. Two of her salient characteristics were a willingness to attempt anything, and kindness. A man who later became club secretary told me recently: 'I still remember my first time out with the club. I was very young and shy. It was Con who made me feel at home.' So perhaps it was not surprising that I tended to seek her out, to ride with her, at first sometimes and then constantly, to sit near her at tea, and, I fear, to bore her terribly. She says that at first I only had two subjects of conversation, rugby football and the odd kind of insurance work in which I spent my business life.

Intimacy developed very slowly. She had an assured way of life, established friends both male and female, and a responsible job in the City as a shorthand-typist. She was also heavily engaged in church and Sunday-school work. Her life, then, had a definite pattern, whilst I was far less mature, far less purposeful.

How does affection begin and develop into love? Perhaps it grew almost imperceptibly, as we tended to turn more to each other than to other people. Maybe the first outward sign was when, meeting on the dark open top of a bus coming home from work on winter evenings, she let me hold her hand. Then, when I left her at her home after a cycle ride, in the privacy of the hall of that quiet terrace house, I would be allowed a brief goodnight kiss. Slowly, slowly, we became closer, but I was nervous about making demands, and she had standards (instinctive, I think, rather than learnt) of what was permitted and what was not. She had the natural shyness of one who grew up in a mainly feminine household. She had no brothers, and her father died when she was still a girl.

In fact, we were both so tentative that it was a warning from her younger sister that I seemed to have serious intentions which made her consider seriously where our relationship was heading. After much thought, she arranged an occasion when we could talk privately, and told me firmly that a special relationship between us could not be considered. (Direct references to marriage, and so on, were avoided.) The main reason, in her eyes, was the fact that she was older by three and a half years. The background, which she never voiced and probably avoided even admitting to herself, was that even at twenty years of age I was very immature, unreliable, and showing little sign of any settled plans for the future. Our talk was painful to me, deeply disappointing, but she made it plain that I must accept the decision, and I did.

I was unhappy to the point of misery for a while. In fact, I did no work at all for three days, staring gloomily at my desk at the office, while a friend and colleague covered up for me. But gradually I adjusted to the position and went on with my usual activities, outwardly normal, or more or less so.

Two months later, I reached my twenty-first birthday. We had a party at home with a dozen or so of our closer friends. Two things about it stand out. One was that Jimmy and M., entirely impromptu, did their own impression (doubtless wildly inaccurate) of a French apache dance, with lots of strutting and stamping. It had us all helpless with laughter.

The other was that Con left rather early, about eleven o'clock. She flatly declined any escort for her walk home, so as not to break up the party. I therefore saw her only to our front door. There, she suddenly turned back, tilted up her face, with a mysterious smile framed between the cloche hat and the fur-collared coat, and kissed me. In a flash she was gone, leaving me gazing at the door, before returning somewhat dazed to the festivities. Had she begun to change her mind?

There was a change in our relationship, but it was still a gradual one. Sometimes I wanted a closer touch than she would allow. Mostly, I was glad just to be with her, even at arm's length. It was all very different from the lightning commitments we are led to think normal in the more sensational fiction today – and which so often end equally quickly, or else slowly moulder away into misery. Maybe it was the slow beginning which helped it to last. It was five years from that 'final parting' on 1st December, 1927, to the other December when we married, and nearly another two before we were launched into parenthood.

Our married life, however, was no millpond. People say that most difficulties in marriage stem from sex or money. We have had few serious problems over money. For a number of years we had very little money to disagree about. Decisions were simple, and priorities usually obvious. Both were helped by a decision not to buy anything on credit, with the exception of a house, and even that transaction came to a premature end for reasons which I need not detail. Later in life we had money, but never in such quantities as to make things difficult. I have seen as obvious cases of people getting into trouble through having too much money as I have of people embarrassed by poverty. And I have also known many who have been happy and content with amazingly little.

We had more disagreements in the general area of sex, but even here the extent of agreement is something I am grateful for. Our two children were wanted, and wanted at that time, which underlined heavily our gratitude for them.

Once I was staying with friends at Namur in Belgium, and was there introduced to a young Catholic couple. During an interesting talk, they suddenly put me very much on the spot by asking what I thought was right as regards the physical side of marriage. Their church had strong rules, which they (like many others) found it hard to follow. After some hesitation, I said I did not feel able to advise them what to do. I believed in absolute purity, but each person had to think out what that meant in practice. I was not always clear about it myself, I said, but I had arrived at two personal convictions which I felt sure about. One was that the primary purpose of our sexual powers was the creation of children, and pleasure was definitely secondary to that. (A similar distinction as regards purposes could, I suggested, be made in connection with eating and drinking.) The second point was that it was wrong for one person to exploit another for selfish ends in this as in all other areas of life. I expected they would say, 'That's not much help', but in fact they said it was very helpful.

Perhaps unselfishness is the real key to a right attitude in these matters.

Glad as I am that we have had a growing relationship now for well over fifty years, I am still very conscious of shortcomings. Sometimes, in moments of despair, I wonder if I will ever understand her, if I will ever learn not to produce wounding words and actions. Too often, even now, we have a difference, and we have to leave it unsolved, or partly unsolved, while we get on with the business of living.

Often my self-centredness, my demanding nature, has been contained, controlled, and even contradicted by what I can only describe as a quality of motherliness. I have just looked up a passage in *Music at Midnight*, the play by Peter Howard and Alan Thornhill. The prime minister has sought and obtained approval from his wife of his broadcast speech which has just been transmitted on television. He goes on teasingly, 'Sometimes I wonder what would happen if you said, "No, dear, it was terrible".' The wife (played by Nora Swinburne in the original production) replies: 'I know just what would happen. I tried it once. You curled up your lip like a boy who's fallen down and is trying not to cry – and you sulked for a week.' The prime minister laughs and says: 'Secretly, you think I'm about ten years old, don't you?' 'No, dear,' replies the wife tenderly, 'At least twelve.'

My wife greeted the passage with a big laugh, what an analyst of humour called 'the shout of delight with which one recognises one's self'. But I have noted traces of the same motherliness in others besides her. Certainly M. had it. So did some of my succession of secretaries – to whom I owe a lot. Now that I am older, too, I enjoy spotting this attitude towards me in those a generation younger, and even two generations younger. It is something to value highly.

Do all women have it in some degree towards all men? Or do they show it only to those who need to be mothered?

Looking back over what I have written in this chapter, I am struck by two things.

One is that the experiences described are pretty superficial, and centred on my own interest in girls, and what aspects of them affected me. It may not be very blatant, but a feminist reading it might well mutter something about women as sex objects, or even 'male chauvinist pig'. That's what comes of trying to be honest about one's reactions.

The other is that there is no appreciation of the sweeping changes between the years of my youth and today in women's attitudes, opportunities, and status in society. When I was getting to know E., V., M. and others, they may have seemed lively, independent and influential in certain ways, but their scope for action and development was strictly limited in the sort of society we had then. In theory, women could do all sorts of things, and a few did become doctors, explorers and so forth, but in practice virtually all women had only limited choices open to them as to the life they should lead. One was domesticity, to be a wife, a mother, a 'daughter at home' if that was necessary. When we married, my own wife unhesitatingly chose this, feeling that her vocation was to be a home-maker, and she never considered having any other occupation or career from that point on. The alternatives in those days were mostly in a relatively limited range of occupations, often involving direct service to others. Women could be shop assistants, nurses, teachers (my wife's headmistress tried to urge most of her pupils in that direction), in certain types of work in offices, in hotel and catering work, and in particular trades and industries such as the garment industry. Positions of authority and influence, in government, the professions, industry, commerce, the leadership of organisations, all were closed to them, perhaps not in theory, but certainly in practice. When were women first allowed to vote, even? Was it 1918?

Slowly, this situation has changed. Today, it is illegal in this country to discriminate against women in matters of employment. However, no one can honestly claim yet that equal treatment is given to the sexes in this field. There are still the remains of centuries of prejudice to be overcome. Indeed, most of us have not yet any clear picture of what women's place should be in society.

To a certain extent, I was forced to think more about it by my own daughter. While she was still at university we had some fairly violent arguments which I can now see were really concerned with the fact that I wanted her life to develop in the way I thought right, and she wanted it to develop in the way she thought right. Since she had clear ideas, and mine were by no means clear, it was not surprising that my views did not prevail. In due course, her life developed in ways I usually found surprising, but which seemed to work. She got married a week after she graduated from university. Since then, she has combined her job (sometimes in employment, sometimes freelance) with running a home and bringing up two children, in a way which commands my admiration and respect. It is a far cry from what was expected of girls in my generation, though I am sure some exceptional women did the same, then and earlier.

Much breath has been expended on women's rights and women's place in society in the last few decades. Ink, too. Some of the voices raised against restrictions have been somewhat strident. Some men have resisted change with arrogance, and to defend their own prestige and power. How should this debate be decided?

If one looks first of all at plain physical capability, there is much closer correspondence between men and women than there is difference. As regards functions, a woman can do everything a man can do except one thing, relating to carrying on the species. In the same field, the woman has a group of related functions which the man cannot fulfil. Apart from that, a woman can do anything a man can do, and vice versa. There are of course differences of degree, women being usually smaller and lighter than men, and somewhat differently proportioned. For sheer power and speed man has an advantage, but in some kinds of dexterity it is the other way. In brainwork, there may be some difference, too, but this is harder to measure. Even in sport, where some measurements are easy, the bigger sex is not always the more successful. Over a period of years, open records for cycling on the road at several distances were broken time and again by an English woman, Beryl Burton. No man could match her. In other sports the gap is narrowing between men's and women's performances. 1986 saw the first woman to play in the annual golf match between the Oxford and Cambridge universities.

Where women are at an inescapable disadvantage in careers as well as in sport is in the disabling aspect of childbearing, that is, in the need to concentrate on the child's needs for some months before and after birth. This means, willy-nilly, breaks in a working life which a man does not have to suffer. How disabling it is depends on how the woman decides, as between motherhood and job. It used to be widely assumed that childbirth signalled the end of a woman's working life. Nowadays, this may be so, but she may choose to return to work within weeks, or she may tend the children until they are of a suitable age (five, ten, fifteen, eighteen?) and then go back to work.

What is more generally important is that now it is no longer assumed that it is impossible, or a second best, to have a woman as a Member of Parliament, a judge, a specialist surgeon or physician, or in almost any kind of highly trained occupation. This change of view is unfortunately still so new that women will tell you they have to be better than the men to make the grade. A friend of mine in government service interviewed last year several candidates for a post as his assistant. There had never been a woman active in that particular field before. Somehow, it was assumed that this area was 'a man's world'. He was surprised when a woman presented herself, agreed with a shrug to consider her, and found her so much better than any of the male candidates that he approved her without hesitation.

It must be admitted that 'the powers that be', consisting almost entirely of men, have carried on a tenacious defence against equal opportunities for women. This still goes on, in fields as different as the trade unions and the law. In both of these and in other fields women in the top ranks are rare. It is only a few years since a woman barrister told me that one of her sex had only two areas of law from which to choose if she hoped to make a living as an advocate. One was criminal law, the other family law, covering divorce and so on. This is gradually changing. One lively young woman was determined to succeed in the Commercial Court, where her father had been prominent in his time. She tried to get a seat in a well-known set of chambers where barristers specialised in commercial work. Every lawyer in the chambers agreed that she should be admitted to their team, but the clerk who managed the chambers vetoed it. She found a place elsewhere, and has been most successful. She, too, seems to have taken marriage and motherhood in her stride, as it were. One story about her might be worth telling. She opposed a request to postpone a case on the grounds that she was pregnant, and would not be able to appear at the later date. The judge referred back to the applicant's barrister who, it chanced, was also a woman. She responded, in effect, 'My Lord, I cannot resist when my learned friend bases her argument on that particular consideration.'

Sex seems to have come back into the picture. This, however, cannot be avoided. The People's Republic of China at one time frowned on make-up or clothes which accentuated femininity, and of course attracted the men. Their womenfolk became an army of dull pale faces and dull blue tunics and trousers. It could not last.

Travellers today tell me that the streets of Chinese cities glow with colour again. But the key to inter-sex relationships, which control the differences between men's and women's roles in society, seems to be the single word 'respect'. If every individual is treated with respect, there can be no question of anyone being confined to an inferior status. Then, too, a proper status can be attached to every person's role. And if this is done, it is much easier for a woman to take on whatever work she feels suits her best.

In a capitalist society, the value of different jobs tends to be assessed by the sum paid to the worker. It seems difficult to avoid this entirely, but it used not to be so. Nurses used to be highly valued socially although very poorly paid. Teachers were in a rather similar position. Most civil service posts drew pay less than that for corresponding jobs in the private sector, partly because of the prestige attaching to being a government servant, but partly also because of the then unusual fringe benefits of permanent employment, long holidays, and a pension. There are hot debates in various fields nowadays as to what should be the pay for various jobs, and a sad result of the passions raised has been the strikes in caring professions where such action would once have been unthinkable. Some of these ills could be avoided if there was less comparison and more genuine appreciation of every kind of work. A pat on the back is no cure for exploitation, of course, but to some people it is more valuable than cash. In fact, we all need that sort of encouragement.

A feature of recent years has been a growth of interest in unpaid or lowly paid work of a charitable nature. Thousands, perhaps millions of people, partake in this, in many countries. Most people have heard of the American Peace Corps, as well as of Voluntary Service Overseas. There is an organisation of French doctors and other health workers which has the knack of appearing in the most distant areas of extreme need, like Ethiopia and Afghanistan.

This may be a further key towards valuing people and their contribution to society on their merits rather than by an arbitrary scale, monetary or otherwise – a necessary step if women (and men, too) are to have full freedom to move constructively into any field they choose. And if we do come to be judged on what contribution each of us makes in a lifetime, that judgement will certainly not be based on the wages earned or the profits made.

13

The Main Streams of Life

The problem about this chapter is that it has to be adequately emphasised, since it fills the gap between two sections of a story, a gap of some fifty years. But it also has to be brief, since I have written quite fully of these matters in the earlier books *Ships that Go Bump in the Night* and *Ships Afloat in the City*. These give a good deal of detail on my unusual working life, and of the changes in my own outlook during that period. So I will summarise these things briefly here, to link the days of my youth with today.

There have been two main streams in my life. One began to flow in 1924, flowed strongly until 1972, and has continued to a certain extent in the years since. The other flooded in in 1933, and has flowed strongly ever since. Their effect in this little area of one person's life is a bit like that on a much greater scale of the White Nile, sluggish, powerful, dense with rich silt, and the Blue Nile, rushing fiercely down from the Ethiopian mountains, which together form that great source of life from the south to north of Egypt. When they join, they run alongside, then overlap, then mingle and become one.

The first stream (into which I was flung suddenly and with little real preparation) was my involvement with a very unusual form of insurance. Marine insurance is the odd end of the insurance market; some would say it is the most exciting and romantic part, some would say the most weird and unorthodox. It is probably fair, too, to say that it is from the marine branch that three new branches have budded off in the last few decades: first came aviation insurance, which still often catches newspaper headlines; then came oil-rig insurance, which produced some entirely novel problems; most recently, there has come the insurance of space satellites and kindred structures, which involves huge sums of money and risks which are very hard to estimate, and in which history is still being made almost month by month.

Marine insurance is still very important and very innovative. Changes are continuous. And if marine insurance is the freakish end of the market, marine liability insurance is the freakish end of the marine market. Back in the middle of the nineteenth century, insurers were so wary of covering the liability risks that shipowners got together in what they called 'clubs' to insure each other for the sums they might get called upon to pay for people who were killed or injured, for other ships and property which might be damaged, and so forth. At first the growth was slow. After a while, the 'clubs' were formally organised as non-profit-making insurance companies, controlled by the shipowners who were insured. They elected a board of directors amongst themselves, and jointly employed a manager or a firm of managers. They became known as protecting and indemnity associations or 'P. and I. clubs'. By 1924, when I joined one as a junior clerk or 'office boy', there were only about fifteen of such concerns worldwide, and in our case the staff was only a dozen people.

However, since then life has got much more complicated. Entrepreneurs such as shipowners have been hedged around with more and more liabilities. Dozens of new countries have developed merchant fleets. The 'P. and I. Clubs' have grown and changed to correspond. There are still only a handful of them, but they have to be able to deal with almost anything which happens to a ship anywhere in the world. Even when I retired in 1972, the list of risks covered had thirty-four paragraphs, each of them covering some class of liability a shipowner might have towards someone else. Our particular 'club' was the largest, and it insured shipowners in seventy countries. Some of these ship-owners were governments, some were huge multinational companies, and some operated from one room in a back street, to run one or two little ships. Most of them are occasionally exposed to possible liabilities running into millions of dollars, and want insurance cover accordingly. But the 'club' may also be called in if a passenger breaks a finger, or a few bags of cargo are misdelivered.

In this colourful and intricate set-up my functions were at first very simple. I added up columns of figures, delivered letters to nearby offices, and tended the smoky coal fires. But when I addressed envelopes I wondered who and what the recipients were in so many countries (even if I did once send off to Dunedin a letter addressed to Dundee). When I showed in a visitor to one of the seniors, I pondered who he might be and what he would be discussing. When I indexed the letter copies, I read as many as I had time for, to see what was going on.

Eventually I did almost every job there was in the office, filing documents, keeping accounts and records, operating the small telephone exchange, typing a little. Then I was allowed to answer some of the letters, dictating at first to the girl telephone operator, and later to a typist allotted to me. Later, I became a sort of general handyman, what might in a larger and more formal firm have been called a manager or even general manager. By then I was handling a big volume of correspondence and I began to travel abroad to sort out problems and see people, first in Europe, then to Australia and other continents. After I was made a partner in the firm, I learnt further skills, the assessment of what premiums should be charged (which insurance men call underwriting), and the management of investments. Sometimes, too, I would sit by the chairman and help him conduct a directors' meeting.

It became a life in which each day would include ten, twenty or thirty varied tasks. Some would be dealt with face to face with colleagues, shipowners, other insurers, lawyers, all sorts of people, some by letter, telephone, cable or telex. There might be drudgery over detail or sudden far-reaching decisions, long negotiation or a free-ranging discussion within a group. It was necessary to grasp medical technicalities regarding sickness or injury cases, engineering matters when machinery broke down or a ship's performance was being analysed, legal niceties when a lawsuit was under way, and a host of other things. It was necessary, even more, to cope with a wide range of people, powerful or retiring, highly intelligent sometimes, and in other cases unlettered and inarticulate. And of course as the office staff grew into hundreds, there were administrative details, too, to distract and confuse.

Simultaneously with this development of my life, from 1933 onwards there was another flow of thinking and activity which was certainly no less important. This also began in a deceptively simple manner, with a conversation with another young man. He talked (as most young people do) of the possibility of a change in the world, but also claimed that it was possible for an individual to change, and that he had begun to experience it. The secret, he said, involved accepting absolute moral standards of honesty, purity, unselfishness and love, and he added something I did not quite follow about receiving guidance. It was rather intriguing.

A few days later he and another young fellow whom we both knew through the cycling club asked me to a meeting near the Tower of London after work. There were thirty or forty men there, and a variety of speakers, from a young office boy to a managing director, talked mainly of their own experiences. Two points particularly registered with me. One was the emphasis on 'guidance', often referred to as guidance from God. This might be experienced by sitting quietly in thought, and writing down what thoughts materialised. The other was that this group was part of a loose and informal collection of people in several countries. Some people were beginning to call it the Oxford Group. Later, it became known as Moral Re-Armament.

The whole thing rather fascinated me. I explained that I didn't believe in God, but the people I spoke to seemed to think this unimportant. I told my wife (we had been married about five months) all about it when I got home. She was impressed enough to suggest that we try out the listening idea the next morning.

So began something which progressively influenced every aspect of my life. It began as quietly as a new leaf unfolding on a tree. There would be a quiet chat, or a few people would meet in someone's house or flat. Each morning we spent some time in silence. I would jot down some notes in a pocket diary, and discuss them with my wife over breakfast, perhaps also with one of the others when we met. If the thoughts suggested some action, I learnt to take it without delay. Yet these inconspicuous moves introduced me to a relationship with God – the God I did not then believe in – which was to open me up to far-reaching and lifelong change.

I could go on to sketch the activities of the years that followed, the recruiting, the training, the major conferences in England, the Netherlands, USA, Switzerland, Japan, involving every class, race and type of person. This would, however, miss the main point, for the activities only reflected a development more subtle and more difficult to define.

I believe Victor Hugo wrote that there is nothing so powerful as an idea whose time has come. It was the development of an idea which progressively gripped me and others during those years. This idea is still developing.

To begin with, the outlines were clear and hard. In considering changes for individuals and change in the world, I expected clear-cut change. Sometimes it very obviously happened, as when a nine years' feud with one of my seniors at work was abruptly ended on an initiative from me, or when the Norwegian Treasury had to open a new section to deal with the results of a widespread stirring of consciences over taxes, following a whole series of meetings in Norway. Similarly, when I accepted in principle absolute moral standards, I assumed that everything would clearly divide into Wrong and Right. This youthful arrogance discounted the need to ponder decisions, and to wrestle with what was the right course in a complicated situation. It also tempted me to stray over at times into a different and deplorable situation, where I began to think that I was Right and They were Wrong.

Again, when I worked at the novel conception of 'guidance', I tended to assume that there would always be a supply of clear unambiguous direction available on request. I would get impatient if no answer was apparent. It needs some maturity to accept that often the guiding message is simply 'Wait'.

It is a matter of history that Moral Re-Armament (or 'moral re-armament', if you think of it more as a principle than as a more concrete phenomenon) was initiated by an American, Frank Buchman. From an obscure beginning he became known world-wide, respected by thousands, both eminent and unknown, in many countries. By others he was bitterly attacked. On his death, leadership was carried on by the Englishman Peter Howard. When he too went, an informal collective leadership emerged, spanning most of the world, and this continues. In the half-century for which I have known this work, it has changed not at all in its basic principles, but constantly in its tactical approach to events.

Buchman, for more than forty years in which he built the work from nothing, and Howard, before his early death, both did all they could to share their responsibilities widely, but without too much success. This could be put down to their outstanding talents, or to the shortcomings of others. Neither had any official position, or an organisation to command. What leadership they took, was taken by consent. Neither of them was an obvious choice for an international spiritual initiative. The American came from an undistinguished background of a small town in Pennsylvania and the Lutheran church. The Englishman left Oxford without a degree, and was trained by Lord Beaverbrook as a hard-hitting, ruthless political journalist. Both, however, not only experienced a great and fruitful personal change, but were also great innovators. For example, in his early years, Buchman was barred from China by other Christian workers, partly for urging that the Christian church in China should have Chinese leadership. Later, Howard put forward advanced ideas in a series of plays, most of which were also filmed, as well as in inspired journalism of a new kind.

Both of them, too, adopted gratefully the ideas of others. Buchman's emphasis on guidance and the four absolute moral standards seems to have been taken over from well-known evangelistic writers of the nineteenth century. When he was much in England in the nineteen-thirties, he often quoted from two widely-contrasted associates of that time. One was Louisa, Countess of Antrim, a former lady-in-waiting to the Queen of England; the other was Tod Sloan, a radical agitator from London's dockland. Later, in 1955, he made a broadcast entitled 'The electronics of the spirit', derived from a dinner conversation in Los Angeles with Lee de Forrest, a pioneer of electronics when most people had not yet heard that word.

Similarly, Peter Howard once gave a sparkling talk to six hundred people in London, including coal-miners and steel workers from Yorkshire and South Wales. I can still remember parts of it, almost word for word. Later that day, I realised that much of it was based on that day's newspaper headlines, and the issues behind them. There was, for example, a science item on the question of the manipulation of genes, and the moral issue of whether man should try to control what sort of babies should be born. And to illustrate how Howard's mind was open for fresh ideas even on a day of concentrated activity, I can add that he stopped me in the street after the meeting to discuss the possibility of chartering a passenger liner as a factor in MRA moves in the Far East.

Howard returned to the question of genes in his play 'Happy Deathday', in which a scientist suggested as a remedy for racial differences a genetic programme which would ensure that all children were blended into a stock of the same colour – 'a universal buff'. About that time, too, a friend of mine was at a meeting where a panel of scientists extolled the benefits mankind would receive if the types and qualities of babies were determined in advance. A questioner from the floor asked what sort of people would they plan for. The spokesman looked at his colleagues and said, 'Something rather like us on the platform here.' How the gods must have laughed! But I regard the whole possibility with horror. Suppose the people who controlled the birth programme decided that everyone in future would be just like me.

In a newspaper statement, too, Howard summarised the problems of industry with almost incredible brevity, and in a metaphor inspired by his practical experience of farming. Too many people, he wrote, were interested in milking one end of the cow, and too few in feeding the other end.

All this swirl of development of the ideas which make up Moral Re-Armament flowed into me and my business activities, as it did into many other people and their activities, in education, medicine, industry, diplomacy, and other fields. I find it hard to separate now the two main streams of my life. Over a business lunch in Karachi, a Pakistani shipowner asked, 'And what are you interested in outside of business, Mr Ledwith?' I mentioned Moral Re-Armament. He said at once: 'How remarkable! My best friend is deeply involved in it, so naturally I am interested, too.' On the other hand, it was at a Moral Re-Armament conference in Switzerland that I first met an Italian shipowner who later became a director of the P. and I. club for which I worked.

In two widely separated countries men I met through MRA became agents for my firm. They were excellent agents. And if my wife and I spent an evening watching one of Peter Howard's plays with a Greek shipping man and his wife, was that MRA or business?

The overlap extended, too, into all sorts of areas. If I tried to practise the absolute honesty and unselfishness my MRA friends spoke of, this directly affected my business life. And the things I learned from the international shipping community equipped me better to grasp the wider implications of moral re-armament. Occasionally (as is the case with many people) there was an opportunity, however slight, to influence national or international affairs, say in the discussions over a new law, or some major agreement. Would pressure for what was right over such an issue be considered as forwarding moral re-armament, or as sound and responsible business practice? Surely it would be both.

Some of the rough edges of my convictions of years ago have been rounded off, but I am even more conscious now of the everlasting war between good and evil. It goes on inside every person every day. My working life, too, was never insulated from it. The war had to be fought there, as everywhere else. I have learned, too, to look beyond labels and formulae, to be alert to the failings of those recognised as good or at least well-intentioned, and to welcome the good done by those who are least expected to do any. Every ally is welcome in this contest, and every enemy can also be seen as a potential friend.

Also, I do believe that the war is being won, even if often progress is grindingly slow.

14

Money

For forty-eight years I worked in what is almost certainly the biggest concentration of money men in the world. The City of London, 'the square mile', roughly corresponds in area with the old Roman and medieval city. Some fragments of the ancient walls still remain. Only a few thousand people live there now. It is almost entirely offices, and predominantly they are those of men concerned with money.

Here are the bankers – the merchant bankers, the head offices of the High Street bankers, the investment bankers, and the international bankers, Americans and Swiss, Japanese and Russian, and from most other countries of the world. Here, too, are the brokers – stockbrokers, shipbrokers, insurance brokers, commodity brokers, and such a variety of others that, though I used to deal with sugar brokers, tea brokers, metal brokers, and a long list of other intermediaries, I am sure I knew only a minority of them. The foreign exchange market in London, where currencies are traded against each other, is (according to *The Times* of London) the world's biggest. So is the vast insurance market of Lloyd's and the companies, or so I have been told by both American and British brokers, over and over again. The net earnings of insurance make a very big contribution to Britain's balance of payments. In other words, they pay for much of the food we eat and the other goods we import. There are, too, a great variety of other people providing specialist services relating to money matters.

A curious feature is that most of these money men, in contrast to popular ideas about them, are not very interested in making money for themselves. If they do succeed in doing that, they enjoy it, of course, but their concentration is much more on the skill, experience and judgement they have to exercise in doing what is often a rather unusual job in that particular niche of the financial world. Profit has its place, but not on such a level as some noisy critics suggest. An international grain broker told me that his firm's target was to make a profit on the total of its deals in any year of one half of one per cent. My younger brother was a foreign exchange dealer. On many of his deals, he was happy to make a profit of one eighth of one per cent. And he was good at his job, though he laughed about the six telephones on his desk, and said it was a bit like being a bookmaker. When he died, most of London's leading dealers came to his funeral, and his employer, with tears in his eyes, told me that my brother had done so well that the plan had been for the boss to retire and bequeath the business to him.

At the time I write, everyone is prophesying an even greater importance for the City of London, and a greater influence for it on the financial setup in the world, linked ever more closely with New York, Frankfurt, Tokyo, Zurich and all the other centres. Yet everyone, I think, who ever considers the point, would agree that there is something gravely wrong with the way the financial system works.

Different people would pick on different aspects of this. Some would point to the huge and increasing gulf in resources between the rich nations of 'the North' and the poor ones of 'the South'. Since this gulf was emphasised by the Brandt Commission, there has been much lip service to the need to deal with it, but what steps have been taken have not been enough even to halt the growth of the gap. Politicians seriously underestimate the scale of the action needed, and both they and the money men are constantly diverted from such large problems to more fleeting issues – that week's slide in value of the pound, the dollar or the yen, an election, or a move in oil prices.

Associated with this North/South divide is the poverty of so many 'Third World' countries, which makes them unable to cope with crises like epidemics, drought or floods. Many of them (and not only the poorest) are overloaded with debts to international bodies, other governments and commercial banks. During the recent famine in sub-Saharan Africa, a statement was made that the many millions of dollars' worth of aid which was poured into certain countries represented less than half what those suffering countries were paying out to service their debts. I distrust such sweeping 'statistics', but it could be true. It is certainly true that several governments, especially in Latin America, have accumulated loads of debt which are ludicrously beyond their ability to carry. Some have in effect defaulted on loans by asking for 'rescheduling', and such requests have been granted for fear that the great jerry-built structure of international credit would collapse.

Other people would complain of different issues. Unemployment has become a blight on almost the whole world. Some say that it is due to lack of investment, and even argue that investment to provide employment must be enforced by governments. If ever that were tried, what funds are available are likely to disappear very quickly. Some also complain of multinational companies switching their operations from country to country, according to levels of profitability. A close relative of mine lost his job in Belgium when the company found it cheaper to concentrate its operations in the United States. But the rights and wrongs of such moves could be endlessly disputed. Every such situation involves different factors.

Destruction of the environment, including pollution by air and water, is often the result of money considerations. The interests involved 'cannot afford' to install expensive equipment to control waste products. Money, too, is behind situations where food piles up in profusion in some areas, while in others hunger is common.

Taxation systems are blamed for many troubles. In detail, this criticism is often right. To correct matters, however, is a slow process either in a democracy or an autocracy, and always the general interest has to be weighed carefully against those of individuals and groups.

Complaints, in fact, are common, and often justified, at all levels down to 'my wages', 'my pension', and even the child's doubts about 'my pocket money'.

I myself have a deep conviction that our whole approach to money has become twisted, so that we forget the main purpose of the money system. Instead, we focus on what is at best a secondary aspect, at worst an evil distortion of what should be. To most of us, most of the time, money has become simply the means of satisfying desires, or of exercising power over others.

I suppose that my earliest exercise in the use of money was when, at the age of six or earlier, I stood debating eagerly with myself the disposal of my 'Saturday penny'. The scene was usually a little dark shop on the short road called 'Tulse Hill Station Approach'. My nose was pressed to the dusty window. My tongue moistened my lips, as I muttered to myself and eyed the sweets in the window, set out on little dishes with a price card on each. For some of the commoner kinds, the strange old lady inside charged only a penny for four ounces, and would weigh them out, shovelling the pieces into a plain paper bag with a little scoop. More luscious varieties might be twopence for four ounces or even more. Should I go for quality or quantity? I usually settled on the cheapest, but it was a matter for grave decision. Sheer self-indulgence was the main motive, though there was also the comforting spiritual feeling if I offered my big brother or small sister, a friend or my mother, a chance to dip into the bag. If I did.

Later, I was equally earnest, equally dedicated to squeezing the utmost in self-indulgence, out of buying the detective novels which appeared weekly, featuring the exploits of Sexton Blake or his slightly down-market rival Nelson Lee. They looked like a cheap magazine, not much more bulky than a child's 'comic', but the close-printed pages contained a long complete novel, illustrated with line drawings and a gaudy cover. How many pence did one cost? Was it three, or four, or even as much as six? (And there were 240 pennies to the pound, then, before decimalisation.) I pursued the accumulation and study of these yarns – and good yarns they were – with a dedication as passionate as that with which Livingstone explored Africa, or the medieval philosophers the secret of transmuting base metals into gold. In fact, I collected such a store of them that they came in useful a few years later. Prior to departing for a seaside holiday at Herne Bay with my father and brother, I found myself very short of spending money. I carried a double armful of Blakes and Lees round to a newsagent who kept a box from which he sold such offerings secondhand (as well as the weekly new ones), and I sold the whole pile to him for no less than ten shillings. That was my first experience of wealth, which was, I fear, soon squandered in ice creams and such.

At Christ's Hospital, too, though our pocket money came in pennies, it seemed vital to us. When the tuck-shop opened in the afternoons, a struggling mass of boys was quickly jammed against the strong wire grille that protected the counter, reaching out coins into the small openings in the wire, and shouting requirements. Doughnuts were, I remember, the most favoured way of filling spaces left by our scientifically calculated meals. In mid-morning, too, between classes, the authorities served out two thick unsweetened wholemeal biscuits, known as 'Housey biscuits'. An enterprising youth in my house used this ration to support an unusual scheme. He turned them into currency. When a new school chaplain was appointed, there was speculation as to how long he would detain the school for his first sermon in chapel. The boy referred to set up as a bookmaker, quoting varing odds in Housey biscuits for all periods from ten to thirty minutes, with longer odds for 'the field' of less than ten, or over half an hour. His net winnings were said to exceed a hundred biscuits from a house of fifty boys; that showed what a crowd of depraved gamblers we were at heart. Some reckless plungers went biscuitless for many days, while the bookie gorged himself happily, and even fed a surplus to his particular friends.

New York friends told me of a somewhat more developed exploitation of money in their family. The youngest son earned the sobriquet of 'Shylock' from his sisters by making lemonade in summertime (doubtless with fruit and sugar begged or filched from his mother) and retailing it to the other members of the family at a penny a glass. He also organised boys for newspaper delivery rounds, and for a winter business of clearing snow from paths and driveways, taking a rake-off from each boy's earnings.

A new dimension was opened for me when, some few years after I started work, I was allowed to deal with some of the firm's correspondence in connection with different claims. I must have been twenty-three or so when this began, at first part-time, for I was also running our filing department with one or two assistants, and also organising new statistical records. It was fascinating to receive a new claim and realise that it was my judgement and the action which I took which influenced whether we refused the claim or paid it, either in full or in part. I also had to decide whether to engage experts to help me, usually a lawyer or a consulting engineer, and agree the fee to be paid to him. Thus, I was using money as a tool or even as a weapon when a dispute arose. This continued for the next forty-odd years, on an increasing scale. Sometimes the amounts involved were quite large. It was not very remarkable, in my later years, when I agreed a fee of a hundred thousand dollars to a lawyer who had won a difficult lawsuit, and thus saved my firm more than a million dollars.

I also added in those later years some additional skills, in managing an investment portfolio of a few millions, and in setting the insurance rates for one of the group of companies which we managed. This last exercise in underwriting I approached with some nervousness, for it is a specialist skill. I collected all the data I could, and for each risk offered I studied closely the sums involved, and the 'exposure' – the likelihood and scope of possible claims, and their probability. At times, too, I was quoting for insurance cover in direct competition with other insurers, and I devised a formula by which I would not treat those competitors unfairly. However, in most cases there came a point where I had to take a deep breath and say, 'That is my rate'. Later, I checked up on myself, and found that of the first hundred clients for whom I fixed rates, only three showed an unacceptably large level of losses. There were also a few whose records were excessively good, and who had to be offered large reductions on renewal. With such a small group of errors, I was clearly a lucky underwriter.

Over the years, I found myself facing again and again, almost daily, a fundamental choice. I had a degree of control over people and events by the use of monetary power. How should I use it? Should it be just for the sake of control, or to forward my own ends, including of course the lust to do a good job and make a success of the enterprise of which I was a part? Or were there principles which needed to rule these issues?

It is not only in business that money is the instrument for exercising power over others. Governments use it over other governments. Some critics of the United Kingdom accuse it (rightly or wrongly) of trying to carry on its colonial policies and 'gunboat diplomacy' into the post-colonial era by other means, the control by monetary pressure. Big financial interests have wide opportunities for influence and control. In this century, the grouping together of most of the oil-producing countries has produced major financial pressures, some direct, some indirect. Some would say that it was high time that these countries broke the control the main users of oil (represented by the great refining and distributing companies) exercised over the oil producers. For a century or so, that control decided prices, production levels, and often even the tax levels of the producing countries, which were in effect tributary states. However, the big leaps in oil prices, justified from some angles, were a mighty blow to poorer countries who depend on oil for transport and to develop industry and agriculture.

Money, too, has been a weapon used between management and labour in many ways. Sometimes one side has been able to enforce its will, and sometimes the other, with money as the reward of victory, as well as the means of it. Occasionally it becomes a hollow victory. A classic example is that of the London docks. Over the years of my working life, I was on the fringe of a long war between employers and workers, which often pressed indirectly on my affairs, with stoppages, delayed ships, and disputes of various kinds. In the past, employers had ruthlessly exploited port workers, not only in London but in most other parts of the world. There was work when ships were in port, and none when they were not, and the uncertainty helped the bosses to keep down wages to a subsistence level. Changes in industrial practices and the growing strength of trade unions altered the balance of power, which was seized and wielded by some leaders of labour who had ideological convictions and the passion which goes with such convictions. Pay and privileges for the workers increased. In some cases, dock workers exploited their strong position in an unscrupulous way. A ship's agent told me of an incident which he said was not uncommon. The leaders of the gangs of men discharging a ship approached the captain on a Friday afternoon, and said that if he would pay them so much extra money, in notes, they would finish discharging by 7 p.m. and the ship could sail on the night tide. If not, she would have to stay over till Monday. The captain paid the hundreds of pounds, so that his shipowner employer would not lose thousands by the delay. Not all the blame rested with the men. The captain knew the deal was irregular, and the men's actual employers (master stevedores or the port authority itself) failed to control them.

Progressively, the London docks became a place where the unions ruled, and the workers prospered. Men whose fathers or grandfathers had worked in the docks for a pittance drove to work in their own cars from the plushier suburbs, and spent two days a week playing golf. Work in the docks was slow, and unexpected delays to ships were common. The 'good days' did not last very long. The shipowners began diverting their ships to other ports where the ships could be handled faster and cheaper, to old ports like King's Lynn and Shoreham, and to the new container facilities at Felixstowe and down the Thames at Tilbury. Within a few years, London's up-river docks were deserted. Thousands of jobs were lost.

If the real purpose of money is not to help self-indulgence, or to give power and authority, what is its real purpose? I see it just as a device, a means of doing something. It is a sort of universal lubricant, which makes everything work, or work better. It can be used to forward what is right, to care for everyone, to provide stability in society and helpful growth.

When one tries to translate this into action, there are immediate snags. First, no one person or group can see the whole of the overall picture. I certainly cannot. Secondly, particular issues look different from different angles. For example, a man I knew well was responsible for the World Bank's first loans to India after the sub-continent achieved its independence. The new republic urgently needed money, and it is fair to say (and not surprising) that every member of the government had plans for his department which he considered to be the most urgent and essential. The World Bank team considered every aspect, and came to a conclusion which was not easy for them to insist on, or for India to accept. It was that the bank would only make a loan if the government gave priority to projects in three areas of effort – agriculture, transport, and hydro-electric power – and used the money exclusively for these purposes. After a tussle, the Indians agreed, and I have never doubted that the bank's conditions were entirely in the Indians' own interests. However, when I once told this story to a group of friends, one of them, a Scottish doctor, exploded with indignation. He had experience of emerging nations, and he argued that it was wholly wrong for outsiders to set priorities. The recipients of the loan should set their own. It was typical, he said, of the arrogance of the wealthy white countries (who of course provided most of the funds of the World Bank) to make such decisions for other people. Perhaps later, after more thought, he would have considered that it was the bank's money we were discussing, and that if it was to be spread over a multitude of schemes, some of them of doubtful value, the loan might never be repaid, and the new republic's finances and credit be severely damaged.

Another example of differing viewpoints can be found in connection with what are sometimes called captive insurance companies. A few years back there was an unsavoury and damaging affair when the managers of certain insurance funds in London made reinsurance contracts passing on risks to an insurance company abroad which they themselves controlled. Huge sums (millions of pounds) were then transferred from the overseas company into the personal accounts of the managers. There is little doubt that it was a criminal fraud, and those responsible have only (so far) escaped arrest by leaving the country, and perhaps partly by the complications of the methods used to cover up the transactions. In the outcry over the scandal, some voices suggested that captive insurance companies should be banned, and in fact certain types of contract have now been banned as far as Lloyd's is concerned. However, it was not the existence of the tied company which was wrong but the few dishonest dealers, and there are hundreds of such companies scattered across the world, which operate openly and honestly. Their functions are perfectly legal, and very useful. The trouble in forming a judgement is in knowing where to draw the line. Suppose an insurer accepts a risk at a premium of five per cent. He then reinsures part of it with a company under his control at four and a half per cent, the difference covering the cost of his administrating the business. What is wrong with that? If he reinsures at three per cent, it should be very good business for the shareholders of the original 'primary' insurer. But if he reinsures it at eight per cent, it might still be wise, if he has had some indication that the risk will turn out to be a very bad one. So in this sphere, too, it all turns on what is the motive for what is done.

The same can be said about the question of bank loans. Are they made for the good of the recipient, or only to make money for the lender?

A lot of rubbish is talked about the value of a free market, about money finding its own level, and so forth. Much of it is a screen for a determination to be free to do what suits one's own interests. To some, it is perfectly respectable to look after one's own interests, even to do so exclusively. It has been said that the function of Britain's Foreign Office is to look after British interests abroad. But is that adequate? Attila might have claimed that he was looking after the interests of the Huns.

Somewhere, we need to find a more reliable guide, if ever we are to reform the money system so that it becomes the effective servant of the true interests of all mankind.

For many years I enjoyed the friendship of a quiet, self-effacing man who told me on one occasion an extraordinary story. His name was Ernest Grimsdale, and he was a grain merchant, dealing (as the head of the family firm) on both the Baltic Exchange and the London Corn Exchange. He bought large parcels of grain and sold them again, often in smaller parcels, as a sort of wholesaler. He also dealt in grain 'futures', contracting to sell or buy at a date ahead at a price fixed in the judgement (or hope) that when the time came the current market price would give him a profit. By trading in futures, he built up a moderate fortune. Then, in a series of deals, he lost it all. Undeterred, he continued, and was halfway to a second fortune when, early one morning, he had a compelling thought to the following effect: 'It is wrong for you to gamble with people's food. Stop dealing in futures.' He accepted this, and had to tell his many friends and associates that he was no longer in that market. He made it plain that it was a personal decision. He was not attacking the futures market as such. In many cases, there are good and compelling reasons for making a fixed price contract for fulfilment well ahead. Both parties take risks by doing so, risks that may be wholly justified. But I am sure that everyone who heard of Ernest's sudden decision gave serious thought to his own motives in business. He continued to be much respected, and till he retired was often asked to act as a senior arbitrator when disputes arose in the grain trade.

Money matters may be just as significant when they are on a much smaller scale. During the 1939-45 war I took on certain responsibilities in addition to my daily work which entailed my being away from home a good deal. The work was unpaid, and I soon found that I was involved in expenses which I would not be able to meet out of my fairly modest income. I got increasingly worried, and eventually told a friend about it. He asked me when the money would run out, and I said at the end of the week. He laughed, and said I had better wait till then to see what happened. I found this less than reassuring, and when he added, 'Where God guides, He provides', my unspoken thought was, 'Maybe so, but will I see it?' The next morning I received a letter from a subaltern in the army, serving some 250 miles away. He said that he had heard of the responsibilities I had taken on, they would doubtless involve me in expense, and he would like to help with that. He enclosed a cheque for five pounds, a useful sum when you could still get a short ride in a London taxi for a silver sixpence. I had to laugh at myself, too, for even as I was telling the friend about my fears, the cheque was in the post.

Why should not every action connected with money be equally well-judged and effective? We live in a wonderful world, in the midst of vast resources. But I am convinced that its creator did not just slap together some raw materials, and leave it at that. The plan included the details of how successive generations of men and women should use and share the resources of the planet. We have to use our wits on that, but it will help if we consider at every point of decision what the overall plan calls for, what is right on this particular issue. This is valid for a billion-dollar investment, or for the proper use of oil and coal reserves, or for whether I put a first-class or second-class stamp on a particular letter.

We need certain tests, perhaps, which we can apply to check the validity of a decision. In money matters, everyone agrees that absolute honesty is desirable. But what about absolute unselfishness? In my relationships with all and sundry, I can rely on my instinct for self-preservation to cover my own interests, so how would it be if in every transaction, small or large, I were to concentrate on seeing that the other fellow's interests are considered? It could act like a Geiger counter, and give a warning mental buzz to indicate the danger of an unfair decision, one which will spell trouble for someone.

But most of all we need to see everything we do, including our decisions over money, as part of an intelligible whole. The work of creation is still going on, and if we co-operate with it by getting our decisions right, this may well have a domino effect over a wider area than we imagine.

15

Perspective

To look back at life when one is around eighty years old reveals a very different picture from what is seen day by day in the struggle for existence and progress. From the crest of a hill, rough pasture looks like a sweep of green velvet, and a tangle of undergrowth and trees becomes a neat and shapely copse.

When my business life ended in 1972, I was surprised to feel relief. I had enjoyed it so much that I had discounted the wear and tear of the daily struggle with problems, the quick switching from one subject to another, the sequence of people to see and tasks to undertake. Suddenly, I was free to choose how much I did, and what I did.

The years since have been by no means empty. The aggregate of activity diminished, but at certain periods I was as busy as ever. I even managed to do some things I had never had time for until then. However, the ability to space out the things to do, and the ease with which I could now say 'no' to projects made for a fine feeling of freedom.

Travel was one element of life which continued, at least for the first dozen years of retirement. In the second half of my business life, I went abroad anything up to ten times a year. Most of the time, it was to do a specific job, to discuss terms for renewal of certain insurances, to investigate or discuss settlement of a claim, to attend a meeting. Less often, it would be to visit all my firm's business connections in a certain city or country, so as to keep our relationship with them warm and progressive. An exception was the four months I spent in India, to initiate new agency arrangements by giving basic training to a group of local insurance executives. But even this had something of the main characteristic of my overseas visits, which was one of hurry, of activities compressed into a minimum of time. I would fly in, carry out what jobs needed doing, share in formal entertaining of some kind,

146

and fly out again. Probably the most acute example was the three days I spent in Bermuda in 1969, which included starting up two new companies, and holding eight different meetings. Even my wife's presence on many of these trips did not make them leisurely. I took too literally the clause in the partnership agreement that I should devote all my time to the business.

I suppose the remarkable thing, in a way, is that I survived all this without obvious loss of efficiency, except for one year when my colleagues thought I was near a collapse, and made me rest for a month.

Post-retirement travel was better. I could not change my style overnight, but by stages the schedules became more relaxed, and there was more time just to be with people. It became clearer and clearer that just to be with people was something that was really valuable. In fact, it had been so throughout my business life, as I built up a network of associates in many countries, a great number of whom became real friends. At a guess, there are over a hundred names still in my personal address book today of people I got to know through business and have known for twenty or thirty years, at least.

Some of our later journeys have been to new places, to Cyprus, Hong Kong, and great tracts of the United States and Canada. But most have been to places where we have been before. Sightseeing has rarely been the object, either before or after retirement, though we have collected memories of some of the great sights, like the Acropolis and the Taj Mahal. Most of the impacts on us have been of personalities, and in scores of cases we were privileged to see people in their natural settings, their own homes. The settings have varied – a fine apartment on Park Avenue in New York City, a worker's crowded flat in Jugoslavia, a tiny retirement 'Unit' for an old lady in Australia – but human warmth and generous hospitality is everywhere the same.

What have been our gains from such travel? Mostly, it is the personal links, the cross-fertilisation of human contacts. It does not seem to have made either my wife or me into a more international type of person. Our attempts to use other people's languages, for example, are elementary in the extreme, and we are conscious of having only a shallow understanding of their cultures. On the other hand, we increasingly enjoy the company of those from other races and countries, and we are eager to learn more of their societies and their backgrounds. A quick dip into our visitors' book for the last few weeks shows names from Canada, Nigeria, Malaysia, Egypt, and black and white South Africans.

In general, however, the more touch we have with other countries, the more conscious we are of our Britishness. This affects us in two ways.

First, it continually amazes us what a deep regard people in other countries have for us British, and how much they expect of us. In India, for example, educated people boast if they have been at schools largely staffed by British teachers (and Irish). At international conferences, it often happens that people turn to the British for an initiative which will bridge a disagreement – and they are very disappointed if the British fail to respond. I have often heard Asians and Africans speak movingly of their countries' debt to some features of Britain which we tend to take for granted – our trade unions, our legal system, our educational institutions, all of which are widely copied. An emir's son from Nigeria spoke proudly of his training alongside British cadets at Sandhurst for service in his country's army. A young Pakistani explained his presence in England as being on a scholarship from his government to continue his study of English poetry. Japanese business executives (though they have achieved so much that we would be wise to study) gain prestige from some months of training in a British office or factory. Surgeons whom I know personally have gone out to demonstrate and teach their skills in West Africa, in Malta, Russia and USA. If we live up to what others expect of us, our country will be a means of civilising the world which no other country will surpass.

The second way in which international contacts drive home my Britishness is in relation to British history. A distinguished Greek lady told me she had a degree in British history from Athens University. She is unusual, but it is very usual to find people in other lands who know a lot about my country's history, and for good reasons feel far more strongly about it than most of my countrymen do. This is not only so with Irishmen, whose knowledge of the evils and errors we have committed in their country is detailed and intense. It is just as painful to hear a Chinese tell the story of the unequal treaties and the opium wars, when the British grew and imported the drug which was illegal in China then, and largely forced the opium habit on the Chinese people at the points of naval guns, and to the great profit of the East India Company, the shipowners and the merchants. Indians may sound less passionate; it is with more resignation but no less pain that they talk of their conquest and three hundred years of domination. But Africans and black Americans, not to mention the black British, can burst out with indignation over the agonies of the slave trade.

In British schools, we are seldom told of the inglorious aspects of our history. Probably all countries exercise a similar selection of what is taught to children – censorship is perhaps too harsh a word. But it is wrong that we should grow up to think that everything in the past was great and glorious. Much was great and glorious, and we should take pride in that. But it needs to be balanced by a knowledge of the other things, if we are to have a realistic relationship with countries which have been our enemies, and races whom we have exploited and despised in the past. It is not enough to say, 'We don't behave like that today.' Sometimes, in fact, we still do. The Englishman's effortless sense of superiority to others is still to be seen, and is still resented. Moreover, even if we have rejected as a national policy many of the wrong attitudes of the past, we continue to profit from them. We include in our 'national heritage' art treasures which were virtually looted from Asia, Africa and South America. We would not have our present level of comfort and security without the wealth we accumulated in centuries of exploitation.

Often, then, it has been a humbling experience to meet and talk honestly with people from other lands. It is equally humbling to find how generous and forgiving they can be towards us. When I acknowledged to a Catholic in Northern Ireland that the troubles in his country were mainly due to England's past mistakes, he said, 'You are altogether too generous to us on this side of the sea.' Several times, Indians have praised to me many of the legacies left to their country by the British Raj – the railways, the postal system, the universities, and even the value of a link language to bridge the subcontinent's fourteen main languages and seven hundred dialects.

If we are honest in exploring our history, and willing to have our misconceptions corrected, we have much to gain. It is chastening but character-forming to realise how far short our forefathers were of those idealised standards that novelists and even some historians have attached to the explorers, colonisers and adventurers of the past. But we can also unearth evidence of fine men and women, noble aims and some permanent achievements. What of today? Some strident voices will scream that Britain's policies consist of self-preservation, exploitation, cynical profit-seeking through arms sales and commerce in all sorts of unhealthy and harmful goods, and of trying to maintain dominance of other lands by subtlety, double-dealing and money, now that we can no longer do it by threat of naval guns. There is just enough truth in this to make one uncomfortable. Is it outweighed by genuinely unselfish concern for the needs of the world? That is for each individual to judge – and for each to use what influence he or she has towards making the balance swing the right way.

Writing is another persistent strain in the development of my life. I have never thought of myself as a writer. What I have produced has been mostly to meet the need of the moment. And those needs have been very varied. Yet a survey shows that over and over again, something or other has had to be squeezed out, to meet a situation, and a fair bit of it has found its way into print.

The first serious bit of writing I did, I think, was an article for the *Post Magazine and Insurance Monitor*, which was considered the most authoritative insurance journal of a general nature. This article was produced not very long after I was gripped by the ideas of moral re-armament. Various groups of us were continually seeking ways to bring those ideas to the attention of individuals and of the public at large. It was a natural follow-up of our conviction that the ideas were valid and of universal application. As someone said at that time, 'If you knew of a cure for cancer, would you keep it to yourself?' Several of the people I already knew as interested in and practising the ideas, were in an assortment of insurance jobs, the deputy underwriter of a marine insurance company, a broker of life insurance policies, and so on. We decided together to see if the various insurance journals would be interested, and one of the interviews we obtained produced a nibble. An assistant editor of the *Post Magazine* said, in effect: 'If you think you've got something relevant to say, get it on paper, and we'll take a look at it.'

It proved quite a task, but I think we did quite well for beginners. Several of us worked on it, but it was generally agreed that it should appear under my name. The title was 'Insurance in a Changing World'. The theme was the basic need for absolute moral standards, and as far as I remember (which is not much, fifty years later) it read well, and had the essential qualities of being suitable for that magazine, and relevant to the thinking of its readers. I do remember that we mentioned how marine insurance began with a group of merchant adventurers sharing the risks of a voyage which would be too expensive and hazardous a venture for any one man, and that life insurance sprang from the concern of certain clergymen for widows and orphans who were left without any financial support.

From then on, I suppose, I have always had half an eye on the Press in all its manifestations, or if not half an eye, a small sector of my peripheral vision. Occasionally, I have been asked to write something. Sometimes, I have submitted items, particularly to local papers. At other times, I have supplied information to papers for them to report if they wished. It is rarely possible for a paper to allow itself to be used for propaganda purposes. However, valid news items are often gladly accepted, if they are considered of interest.

I even had a paragraph or two printed in the diary column of the *Daily Telegraph*. This was because I knew slightly the man who in those far-off days used the pen-name of 'Peterborough', as other compilers of that column have done before and since. The man in question was George Christ (pronounced with a short 'i'), who was at school with me at Christ's Hospital. I fed him shipping items. He was a lively character. He must have been a year or two older than me, for he reappeared at the school, before I left, on the annual sports day. A regular event was a 220-yards race for old boys. On the spur of the moment, Christ took part in this, wearing a city suit, complete with bowler hat and rolled umbrella, and finished second. Later, in Fleet Street, he caused a minor sensation by giving up alcohol. He told me that he was given a hard time with criticism, even abuse, by his hard-drinking friends, until he retaliated by loudly accusing every critic of being narrow-minded. He was a good journalist, whose premature death was much mourned.

A much more lasting relationship was the friendship I developed with one of the shipping journalists. We took in three shipping weeklies at the office. The most authoritative was called *Fairplay*. Apparently, it had been started about 1880, and the men involved were arguing about what to call it at an informal meeting at the home of the paper's principal instigator and shareholder. His wife was quietly sitting outside the circle with some needlework. When the discussion got nowhere, she observed: 'Well, you are always saying that all the shipping industry needs is fair play from the government, competitors and so on, so why don't you call it "Fairplay"?' The paper was very conservative in policy and in appearance. For example, it would not publish any illustrations (except in advertisements), so that the editorial columns were solid areas of type for decades after its competitors' pages were studded with half-tone pictures of ships, people and places.

For years its editorial staff consisted of two experienced journalists, who more or less split the paper between them. The editor had general responsibility, including the regular weekly articles on the freight market, detailing the rates paid for carrying particular cargoes and for the time charter of ships for longer periods, on marine insurance developments, and on ship sales, with the actual prices paid when ships changed hands. The main text, however, was a sort of editorial-cum-causerie entitled 'The Look-Out Man', which was written or compiled for many years by C.T. Birdwood. This usually covered a dozen or so pages, with cross-headings for different subjects. It could include news, comment, and correspondence, and its quirky and varied contents reflected the character of the man responsible.

His given name was Christopher. Some called him 'Jack' – I don't know why – but he encouraged me to call him 'Birdie'. Again, I don't know why. I suppose that I met him for lunch or coffee about once a week for a long span of years, including the war years of 1939 to 1945. Our talk, like his writing, covered a wide range of matters. To speak directly to him of moral re-armament was usually counter-productive. To grasp his attention, it had to be incidental to his interests of the moment. Sometimes I could give him shipping information or anecdotes. Sometimes we would argue some issue, a process he always enjoyed.

Once he printed in his column some doggerel verses criticising the P. and I. clubs, verses written, I suspect, by an insurance man who had been worsted in an argument, but quite clever and amusing. I constructed an answer to them in similar rhyming couplets, which he was delighted to publish. Alas, the orginal attack has surfaced occasionally since, once a decade or so, and at least once in America. But my reply has sunk without trace. Another time, *The Look-Out Man* published a major and long-running discussion in letters on the future of the shipping industry. One of the first correspondents was Colonel Denis Bates, then chairman of the Cunard Steamship Company, and he wrote again in the closing stages. I contributed a letter, and also arranged (through the wide contacts I had made in connection with Moral Re-Armament) for letters from two men serving at sea, a lower deck rating, and a ship's officer whose experience had included three torpedoings.

Fairplay reported fully, a few years after the war, a fairly major initiative for Moral Re-Armament, involving the sending of a hard-back book to five thousand of the top men in British industry, with a covering letter from five nationally known figures. I worked on this project, but did not myself approach Birdie or his colleague the editor for publicity about it. Copies were sent to the paper in a routine manner. I did, however, gather from hints dropped over coffee that there had been quite a discussion before the *Fairplay* report was prepared. I happened to note that the issue of the paper in which it appeared also contained advertisements by firms headed by three of the five signatories of the book's covering letter. Editorial decisions are, I believe, rarely affected directly by advertising considerations, but the coincidence may have convinced Birdie and the editor of the responsible nature of the move that was recorded.

Birdie also used to introduce me to some of the varied characters he met. I missed him a lot when he eventually left *Fairplay*'s dusty office in Palmerston House for a well-earned retirement.

I also wrote our P. and I. club's annual reports from, I think, about 1933 to 1969. In the later years, colleagues shared the work with me. These were not the formal statements required of companies by law, but booklets which reviewed the year's work in some detail, and commented on current issues of concern to the shipowners. For the club's centenary in 1969, we found with some difficulty contrasting pictures of two ships for a cover in colour. One, which we had insured in 1869, was owned by a Member of Parliament in Sunderland, who was one of those accused by the famous Samuel Plimsoll of sending crews to sea in overloaded 'coffin ships'. Plimsoll was a hot-headed individual, and in respect of this man he was entirely in the wrong. The shipowner sued Plimsoll for libel, and only failed to recover massive damages through a technicality. If he had succeeded, Plimsoll would have been bankrupted, and might never have succeeded in his campaign for governments to control the weight of cargo which each ship could carry. In fact, we might never have had the Plimsoll Line marked on every ship's sides. As a contrast to the Sunderland ship, the booklet showed a newly built container of the Atlantic Container Line, one of the first purpose-built ships for what was then a new trade. She was a sister ship of the *Atlantic Conveyor*, later sunk in the Falkland Islands campaign.

Other technical writings appeared in various forms, as well as various documents relating to moral re-armament, and some which, I suppose, reflected both. A lecture I gave for the Insurance Institute of London on 'The Place of P. and I. Clubs in the Insurance Market' was still in print after thirty years. Later came my two books (and now this third) and all sorts of oddments. They included two articles for the Charles Lamb Society; that engaging essayist and poet has a special attraction for me, not only for his charming character, but because we went to the same school. He was only one hundred and thirty years senior to me.

My involvement with the Charles Lamb Society arose very casually. I was talked into joining it by my neighbour at a dinner for old boys of my school. I vaguely knew that there were quite a number of literary societies around, mostly devoted to studying the works of some writer of the past. And at school, Lamb and his contemporary and fellow-poet Samuel Taylor Coleridge were talked about as our most famous 'old boys'. Everyone seemed to know Coleridge's poem 'The Ancient Mariner' and the fragmentary 'Kublai Khan'. Nearly as many knew Lamb's lament for his youth: 'All, all are gone, the old familiar faces'. I was later to learn that he wrote it at the advanced age of twenty-four! But Lamb's most popular work was his *Essays of Elia* which, it was said, revived English essay-writing to a level equal to the peak of Francis Bacon, and influenced many writers since. The school still honoured his memory with 'Lamb Essay Prizes' every year, and I actually won one of these with an enthusiastic, gossipy piece on the subject of roads.

I found that the Society met six or eight times a year for people to read papers on Lamb's works or those of his circle, or some other aspect of that era (1775 to 1833). Moreover, there was an emphasis on 'preserving the spirit of friendliness and humour that was characteristic of Lamb', actually as one of the objects of the Society. The main event of the social programme was an annual lunch, but there were occasional outings of other kinds.

I hope all other literary societies are as pleasant as that which honours my schoolfellow. It does comprise a very nice crowd of people, and I cannot help feeling that some of Lamb's qualities have rubbed off on them a little. He was a man of deeply cultivated mind, but unassuming and notably good company, at least as much so as the great Dr Johnson a couple of generations before him. But where Sam Johnson held forth weightily and wittily after dinner at an inn or at some great house, Lamb was always entertaining his friends, mostly at his own modest home, sitting and listening quietly, but occasionally convulsing the company by stammering out an outrageous pun. One interesting pointer to his character was his reaction to the frightful episode when his elder sister Mary, in a frenzy of madness, killed their mother with a table knife. To prevent Mary being confined in the primitive mental hospitals of the time, Charles, only twenty-one years old, undertook to look after her, and did so until he died. She kept house for him, and looked after his friends, and he encouraged her too to write, except when an attack took her and she must be confined until she recovered. A second less striking but important pointer to his character is in his relationship with William Wordsworth, the dominant literary figure of his day. Each time a new collection of William's poems appeared, Charles wrote to him, often suggesting how they could have been better. And in the second edition, the proud and reserved Wordsworth would almost always have revised his work accordingly.

Lamb's own work included journalism, essays, and verse. He even wrote a play, which was unsuccessful, and at the first night he characteristically joined in the hissing from the audience.

Much of the academic work of the society is out of my mental scope, but the members, a mixture of academics and those from miscellaneous other backgrounds, and of all ages, like to lace serious research with lighter matters. Someone suggested that I attempt a paper, so I did some reading and produced a fairly detailed comparison of Christ's Hospital in Lamb's time with what it was like in mine, in the more recent past. The first was well documented by Lamb himself, by Coleridge, Leigh Hunt and others. For the second I relied on memory. It was cheerfully received, especially the comparative pictures of the food for the boys (more plentiful in the later era, but with tea at breakfast instead of small beer) and corporal punishment (lessened, but still present and not resented). A year or two later, I tried again, describing the East India Company, where Lamb worked as a clerk for much of his life, and the work he did there. The old East India House, where he began to work at the age of seventeen, had stood only two hundred yards from the office in St. Mary Axe where I also began at seventeen, over a century later.

Such a society takes its character, of course, from its members. Some are overseas, as far away as Japan and Korea, and many American universities subscribe to get the Bulletin's thoughtful articles, but the permanent core in England is as convivial a group as any I have met. A guest at one of the annual lunches described it as 'a very civilised occasion'. My friends, I salute you!

Another repetitive pattern besides travel and writing has been the acquisition of knowledge. As is well known, London taxi-drivers are not allowed to take up the job without acquiring a great body of information on the whereabouts of streets and individual buildings, offices, clubs, and how to get from one to another in this enormous city. They call this 'the knowledge', and the police examine them closely about it before the special licence is issued. On Sundays, it is common to see potential drivers touring London by bicycle or moped with a clip-board on the handlebars, studying 'the knowledge'. When I was a small boy, according to my mother, if I found a dropped tram-ticket on my way upstairs, I would stop and read every word printed on it, before completing the ascent. Certainly, I seem to have an inexhaustible hunger for information.

This was reflected in several ways in my business life. I constructed some of the firm's early experiments in filing and cross-indexing information, using thumb-indexed books and card indices which were crude indeed compared with today's computerised information retrieval, but important to us. In later years, I always had two personal reference books in a handy drawer of my desk. One was simply for names of people, those who came to see us or to whom we wrote or telephoned. With the larger firms, all the different individuals we dealt with would be listed, so that if one was unavailable I could at once ask for another. The second book was what used to be called a 'commonplace book', but adapted for the job. It contained references to key legal decisions, technical data which I needed to be sure of if I quoted it, notes of where various facts could be found in reference books, or in someone else's mind. To give just one example, it included the names of the men at the Atomic Energy Authority who, if telephoned, could tell me whether a particular cargo shipment of a nuclear nature was hazardous or not. I once asked the Authority about a cigarette-making machine – a huge and elaborate thing – which was being shipped to the Middle East. Somewhere in the midst of all the detailed equipment was a radio-active gadget of some kind. Its function was to meter the cigarette paper as it went through the rollers, and to stop the machine if the paper was too thick or too thin. Was it dangerous, I asked. 'About as dangerous as the luminous dial of a wristwatch', was the reply.

When I was training young executives, I urged them always to keep two books like these, and to use them daily. The one with the names was the more important. It matters so much to people if you remember their names, and it is even better if you can refer by name to their immediate family. The fact that you looked it up in your book before you telephoned is not in the least important.

What sort of knowledge was I interested in? Anything and everything. The oddest of scraps of information can prove valuable. Early in World War II I found myself at a reception talking with the chairman and managing director of an aircraft factory. He said that the most active trade union leader in the works was a Communist, who had boasted to him that he could stop the whole factory if he wanted to, even over the price of a cup of tea in the works canteen. And when the price was put up a short while later, the threat was carried out. Even with a war on, and aircraft urgently needed, they had constant stoppages of work, until Hitler invaded Russia. The Communists changed their policy overnight. Instead of opposing a 'capitalist war', they called for total support of their Russian brothers, and all industrial disputes were ended. It was for me a revealing glimpse of the power of an ideology.

At a later stage in the war, at a somewhat similar reception, an American opened my eyes to the growing importance of high technology. He came from the Sperry Corporation. I raked into the back of my brain, found a stray fact, and said, 'Ah, the Sperry gyroscope.' Many other different things, he countered, and started telling me about one of their recently developed gadgets. The high-flying aircraft of the US and British air forces were not then pressurised like modern airliners. The aircrews had to use oxygen masks at high altitudes, and occasionally the oxygen system would develop a fault. Unfortunately, a symptom of oxygen deficiency was euphoria, which meant that the pilot might be feeling fine, in fact very cheerful indeed, just when he was about to die from lack of oxygen, and needed urgently to drop to a lower altitude. The gadget would continuously monitor the airman's blood stream, and, if the oxygen content fell, it would set off visual and audible alarms.

Two other wartime incidents were both connected with Poland. Among the foreign shipowners working from offices in London at that time were one or two Poles. I got to know one of them fairly well, not least when one of his ships was sunk, and we had to deal with survivors, and put money aside for compensation after the war to the families of men who were killed. The incident I most remember about him, however, took place the day after the newspapers reported the Yalta Agreements, when Stalin, Roosevelt and Churchill discussed arrangements for the closing stages of the war, and what should be done after hostilities ended. I boarded a bus in Bishopsgate, and found myself sitting next to this neat, quiet-spoken man. I asked him what he thought of the agreements. The newspapers had described them as an advance in international co-operation. He said, in his soft, slightly accented voice: 'We have lost the war. You declared war to save Poland. Now you have given it to the Russians. My family are there. I will never see them again.' I could say nothing, and sat in silence.

At about the same period, Birdie phoned me from *Fairplay* to ask if I would be interested to meet a Polish fighter pilot serving in the Royal Air Force. We met for lunch at the Great Eastern Hotel. He had an extraordinary story to tell. Like his shipping compatriot, he spoke excellent English, quietly and unemotionally. He had been about seventeen or eighteen at the time of the 1939 non-aggression pact between Germany and Russia. When the Nazi forces invaded Poland a few months later, the Russians occupied the eastern part of the country. All the able-bodied males in his area, including him and his father, were rounded up and shipped off to the Arctic north of Russia, and set to work digging a canal. The work was fairly hard. Each man had to shift so much earth each day. If he could not do so, usually from physical weakness, his rations were reduced below the level necessary to keep him alive. It was considered economically unsound to feed him. One day, in midwinter, the entire work-force in this particular labour camp were marched some kilometres through deep snow to another camp to be de-loused. They had to strip, so that their clothes could be disinfected by baking, while the men went through the baths. By an error, the furnaces were turned up too high, and all their clothes and boots were destroyed. There were no spares on the spot, so they were marched back to camp naked in twenty degrees of frost. Many died. Later, Hitler attacked Russia, and the Soviets and the United Kingdom became allies. One of the many agreements they made on mutual help was that any Poles in Russia who knew how to fly would be sent to Britain to join the air force. His camp records showed that he had had some flying training in Poland. He was extracted from the camp, and flown to Scotland. In telling the story, he was at great pains to emphasise that there had been nothing personally vindictive in what happened in the camps. It was the system. That was all. And for him the system had eventually worked favourably. He liked it in England, and was delighted to have a chance to fight. But the system had not had good results for his father, who was not strong, or for many others.

These two incidents, even more than the talk with the aircraft manufacturer, deepened my conviction of the power of an ideology. In those war years, we were all more or less conscious of the Nazi ideology, which had so gripped a nation possessing great gifts and talents (think of its music as just one of them) and diverted it into vicious ways. In the years since, we have seen, and to some extent have analysed and assessed, the effects of the Marxist-Leninist ideology. But does a compelling idea, an ideology, necessarily have to be divisive and destructive? Surely not.

I once met Vladimir Bukovsky, who was expelled from Russia and now lives in England, and I treasure a signed copy of his magnificent book *To Build a Castle*, on his experiences in the prison camps and psychiatric hospitals. Interviewed on television by Bernard Levin, he claimed forcefully that 'no one in Russia believes in Communism now'. I have met a few Russians and argued ideology with one or two of them. Some are cagey on certain subjects, but all those I have met have seemed attractive people, mostly with an agreeable sense of humour.

A friend of ours threw a party at his house, so that two Russians over on business could meet a mixed group of English people, including my wife and me. At one point, I found myself in talk with the two from Moscow and a Labour Member of Parliament. One of them raised the question of the general election due to be held shortly, and asked the MP what was likely to happen. She replied that it was difficult to say; it might be a close thing, 'but I think we'll just scrape in'. I commented that I had read in *The Times* that there was also to be an election for the Supreme Soviet, and I rather mischievously asked what was likely to happen in that election. The senior of the two Russians appeared to ponder a moment, and then said, 'Well – I think we will just scrape in.'

I was once asked to speak at a special dinner in Hong Kong of my experiences with moral re-armament in business. Most of the guests were local business people, but two were journalists from the People's Republic of China. Afterwards, they thanked me warmly, and bought several books to study.

Maybe the apparent ideological gulf between the Communist and non-Communist worlds is not unbridgeable, after all.

One problem about having such a thirst for knowledge is what to do with what you collect. How do you store it, arrange it, bring it forward when you need it, even know when to discard items which are superseded by new items or which prove to be useless? I have no real answer to any of these questions. Mainly, the reason is that my style of living does not allow time for an elaborate personal filing system. I make do with a few standard aids like a dictionary, thesaurus, a dictionary of quotations, and a medium-sized library of maybe two thousand books. The rest is in my head, and therefore tends to be a dump of miscellaneous information. Only too often, if I want something, the process of recovery becomes something of a mental lucky dip.

The one subject on which I do spend energy to maintain a certain basic organisation of data is as regards people. By this is not meant a series of dossiers, but the bare minimum of data, names and addresses and sometimes very brief notes. And the reason for this is that contacts with people have seemed more and more important as the years go by. They form the framework round which the whole of life is built up. Our address book is therefore a bulky volume, and in daily use. And most of the entries in it represent a degree of involvement in other people's lives, their problems, and their hopes for the future.

These are some of the persistent patterns in these decades of living, but the most important pattern, perhaps, has only emerged into my consciousness as I have written these notes. It seems to me that there has been a whole succession of influences which in different ways, some bluntly, some subtly, urged me to accept and follow absolute moral standards. First, of course, came my parents, my mother bluntly influencing me and my father subtly. Then there was school, especially Christ's Hospital, with already nearly four centuries of tradition to back its attitudes towards the various issues of daily life in those formative years. Then there were the healthy activity and the code of conduct in the cycling club, the Scout movement with its simple moral law, and the girls and women (dominantly, of course, one girl-woman) who expected me to behave correctly with them. The whole process makes me think of the recurrent floodings which in time produce the rich alluvial sediment of a river valley. For nearly twenty years I lived in the Thames valley, where some of the farmers growing vegetables, salad crops, and such, often take three crops a year from their fields.

To these one can also add persistent work in a well-run business, where one was always conscious of being part of a 'service industry'. Some use this expression condescendingly, as denoting a less significant or secondary marginal sort of activity, not so important or so basic to human development as farming or manufacturing, the actual production of goods. I balk at this conception. To my mind, every industry is a service industry. It exists to meet a need in certain people – or else it is wrong, and should be scrapped.

The soil was thus prepared for the formal and direct challenge to absolute moral standards I received from the people who later accepted the label 'Moral Re-Armament'. Over fifty years after I first staggered under the impact of that conception, I am still struggling to understand it. How can a person be absolutely honest? We don't understand ourselves well enough to give a clear picture of ourselves to others. And the more I think about an issue, the harder it seems to me to give a straight answer to a straight question – if one ever gets a question which is not loaded in some way, even from a small child. The most we can hope for is to be as honest as we possibly can – but the aim still needs to be absolute honesty. What is absolute purity? I could not possibly define it. I can only grope towards it. But I do know, of course, some things which are definitely not a part of absolute purity.

The same sort of mental struggles arise over absolute unselfishness and absolute love. Everyone knows about turning the other cheek. It took an Irishman, George Bernard Shaw, to show there was much more to this than mildly submitting to evil. In *Androcles and the Lion*, one of his most stimulating plays, the sceptical Shaw throws more light on Christianity than most Christians manage to do. I particularly like the scene where one of the small group of Christians who are to be thrown to the lions, the brawny Ferrovius, is taunted by an effete Roman patrician, who slaps his face and invites him to turn the other cheek. Ferrovius turns the other cheek and is slapped again. He then rolls up his sleeve, displaying a forearm like a York ham, and says, in effect, 'And now you do it.' Androcles, the sensitive little animal-lover, says, 'Easy, Ferrovius, easy: you broke the last man's jaw.' The giant replies, 'Yes; but I saved his soul.'

Something of this has figured in my own encounters with wrong. I can often do wrong myself, and usually (I hope) admit it. When I come up against wrong in others, as I often have done in business, I hate to see evil victorious. It does not seem to be good for a bad action to be profitable, if this can be prevented. But I never broke anyone's jaw.

In fact, it is far better to prevent the wrongdoing. For this reason, I accepted the other argument of my friends who proposed absolute moral standards – that the unselfish, and indeed the loving, thing was to do all in one's power to get those standards universally accepted and applied. This was and is a programme of ridiculously vast proportions. This makes it even more necessary and sensible to attempt it. The conception came to Frank Buchman in an extraordinary way. It was in England in 1921, and it must be remembered that Buchman had for years set time aside each morning to seek the guidance of God, and was also alert for signs of such guidance at any time. He was cycling along a street in Cambridge late one evening, when the thought came to him, 'I will use you to remake the world.' He was so shocked that he nearly fell off the bicycle, and it was three days before he had courage to tell his associates of the experience.

At that point, he had worked in China and India as well as in America and Europe, but this idea was of an entirely different order of magnitude. He took it seriously, humbling though it was. Of course, he failed to achieve it in his lifetime. Yet it may be that by the time he died the work he started had at least touched every country in the world. Certainly (as far as I can check) it has done so by now. And in some countries, on some issues, important changes have developed. In a few cases, such as the post-war *rapprochement* between France and Germany, the influence of this work has even been officially acknowledged by governments.

In such a programme, there was room for everyone who was willing to help. At first, as I have explained, I was full of enthusiasm and no doubt made myself intolerable to some people by pressing my half-baked ideas on them, in and out of season. But it soon became clear that what we were out for could only be defined as a revolution by consent. To change the world by means of a change in people was only possible if people wanted to change. Therefore my part, and that of my friends, would only be to make the possibilities known, and to provide opportunities for others to join in.

Two examples may help. I think it was in 1959 that I was at the big international conference which was mounted for most of the summer at Caux in Switzerland, and found myself at lunch one day with Victor Laure, a former merchant seaman and seamen's union official from Marseilles. He was an oldish man with a dark, seamed face, and (although I found him an impressive character) it was more remarkable than I then realised that he was so totally dedicated to the concept of a God-centred revolution by consent. He had been a convinced Marxist. I did not know then what life could be like in French industry. It could indeed be a battle. A shipyard worker from St Nazaire told me on a later occasion that once the workers there had only persuaded their employers to discuss a claim for increased wages by burning down the management offices. Not much later, a similar deadlock was only broken by the workers burning all the management's cars.

Victor and I found much to talk about in our different experiences with merchant shipping. We both cared a lot about the industry to which we had given many years of work. Somehow the idea emerged, 'Why not have a special session here in Caux for the world's merchant shipping industry?' We consulted our Swiss hosts who were responsible for the conference centre. They were willing enough, but suggested it would be more effective it if were set up as part of the general conference. The shipping men could then rub shoulders with those of other industries, or from education, politics and other backgrounds. The problems of human nature and the need for change were common to all. We fixed on a period a month ahead, and began to pass out invitations to anyone we thought might be interested.

Humanly speaking, it was a foolish scheme, shockingly badly organised. Despite the wealth of contacts which I had in the international shipping industry, none of those I invited came, though of course I returned to Caux myself. But by various means, there gathered some thirty people in shipping from a dozen different countries. There was even a man from Korea. Strangest of all, there was a group of eight representing management and workers sent officially from the most prestigious shipping line in Germany.

The days went past, and nothing very noteworthy seemed to happen, except when a leader of the Italian stevedores addressed one of the main meetings of the conference. He got on to the subject of pilferage of cargo from the docks. He emphasised that of course he had never been involved in it himself, but went on to describe how big a problem it was, and how difficult the authorities found it to cope. Carried away by enthusiasm, he made it increasingly plain that he not only knew all about it, but for years had been getting away with all sorts of goods. And he ended up with a resounding decision to set an example himself towards putting an end to pilferage in future.

In general, however, there were no signs of concrete developments from our shipping friends. On the last day, we arranged a farewell tea-party for the German group, in a private room with a special cake and so on. Several people made polite speeches. Then one of the management representatives got up, made a short statement in German which I did not understand, and offered his hand to one of the workers' representatives, who jumped to his feet, and shook it vigorously. The whole group were clearly staggered by this development.

I found that the first man had been a fanatical Nazi, and some considered that he had never really given up his former ideas. The second was a known Communist (although the Communist Party was then banned by law in Germany). They loathed each other, and there had been constant trouble in the company in which this personal and ideological antagonism affected all kinds of issues. Over that table of tea and cakes they ended their feud, and as far as I know they did it permanently. So our shipping session did achieve something.

The second example begins even earlier, in the winter of 1938/39. When the conception of 'moral re-armament' was first launched, it was quickly taken up by a wide range of people, by Queen Wilhelmina of the Netherlands, by Muslim leaders in some of the Arab countries, and so on. One man who responded in this way was the then mayor of Battersea in South London. That local government area had 150,000 inhabitants, many of them poor, and mostly of Labour sympathies in politics. In fact, the first Communist Member of Parliament to sit at

Westminster, Mr S. Saklatvala, represented Battersea. Councillor Bill McIver, the mayor that year, responded in this way (I heard him say it): 'I think this is a good idea, and I ought to do something about it. We'll have a public meeting in the town hall, and I'll invite all the voluntary organisations in the borough. Shall we say Thursday week?' It was remarkable evidence of a peculiar English institution. Every town and city (and every section of London known as a borough) has a mayor elected for a year to chair the meetings of the council which governs local affairs, but he is also regarded for that period as the First Citizen of the town. Bill McIver was a retired railway worker, living on a small pension in a little terrace house after a lifetime of hard and badly-paid work. But he was a respected man, and the mainly Labour council had elected him mayor for the year.

A few of us helped with arrangements for the meeting, especially as regards speakers, and we also called on as many of the sixty-four members of the council as we could in the short time available, to let them know what was brewing. With one of the local clergy, I called at several houses. One of them was that of Alderman A.A. Rignall, who is in a sense my second example. He was out, but his wife said she was sure he would attend, to support the mayor. Rignall, always called 'Tim' after Dickens' character Tiny Tim, because of his short but very sturdy frame, was one of the youngest members of the council. He duly turned up but had to leave halfway through the meeting to speak at a local meeting of the Labour Party. There, someone attacked the mayor's action in calling a meeting for the moral re-armament. Tim got up and vigorously counter-attacked, mainly out of loyalty to the mayor, for his knowledge of the subject was confined to the opening speeches he had just heard.

There was such a crowd at the mayor's meeting, including twenty or thirty members of the council, that we decided to have a follow-up meeting for people who might like to look into the matter further. I was again one of the pair who called on the Rignalls, and this time found them both in. Tim, just arrived from work – he was a steel construction worker – was in rolled-up shirt-sleeves, displaying a mighty pair of biceps. He was about thirty then, I think, or a little more. As we sat at the kitchen table, shelves behind his head showed rows of the red-covered volumes of the Left Book Club. Later he told me he had been attracted to Communism, but never quite convinced by it. His wife, fair and with rather delicate features, told us they had one little girl. They both said they would come to the meeting. We asked if they would like to say anything, and it was Lilian who replied that Tim would be sure to have something to say, but she definitely would not.

The meeting came round, and Tim certainly had his say with a real fighting speech of support, partly fired, I think by the imprudent criticism he had encountered from the man at the Labour Party meeting. As he sat down, Lilian caught my eye, and I winked at her. Immediately (and I think to her own and Tim's surprise) she jumped up and declared that she entirely agreed with her husband. We had a secretary taking down a summary of the meeting. Going over her notes afterwards, we decided there was some news interest there, so we put together a short report, and submitted it to the local paper. A long time afterwards, Tim said to me, 'After that second meeting, I knew I'd have to get involved in this some time, but when I saw the report in the *South Western Star*, I knew I'd have to get involved right away.'

At the second meeting, too, I made a tentative date to bring my wife to meet them. It needed some arranging, as our second child was only a few weeks old. She hit it off with them at once, and as we sat at the same kitchen table, Tim plucked up courage to make his first experiment with absolute honesty. He said, 'You know, Lily. Those late meetings at the town hall. Some of them weren't as late as you think. Sometimes there was time for a couple of games of billiards afterwards.' Literally, her jaw dropped. It was only because it was so important that I did not laugh.

Not long afterwards, Tim got the conviction that he should tell his party leader on the council of the new basis on which he was living. F.C.R. Douglas, the leader of the Labour group, was regarded by many as a stern disciplinarian, and an austere and withdrawn sort of man. After the war, with Labour in power in Westminster, he was made Governor of Malta and given a knighthood. Tim made a date, and asked me to go with him for moral support. Naturally, I was grateful for this sign of his confidence in me, though I found the situation rather piquant. My father had been a Conservative councillor in the next borough, and although I had never been involved directly in politics, my background was very much of 'the other side'. Douglas had a flat near Battersea Park, where he lived, practised as a solicitor, and did his council work. I remember his sitting-room as dimly lit, probably dusty, and with papers everywhere. I sat inconspicuously in the background while Tim told his grey-haired leader that in future he intended to seek guidance from God on decisions, in the light of absolute moral standards. He implied (but did not say) that this would rule his council work, even if it clashed with party political decisions. Douglas listened intently, and quietly said something like, 'Well, Tim, I hope you and I will never differ as to what is right on any issue.' When we regained the street, Tim's relief was obvious. He stood in considerable awe of the man who kept in order a big group of varied personalities.

Some days later, Tim had the thought that he should also tell his decision to the leader of the Conservative opposition, and again I was asked to go with him. The small opposition group fought an unending rearguard action in the council. It was an article of faith with the Labour majority that the Conservatives were utterly wrong on every issue, and to hear even a man like Tim speak about them, you would expect to see them fitted with horns and tails. The time came when we opened the gate of a neat little villa off Clapham Common. The leader of the Conservative, Captain Abbott, had another of his councillors with him, a rather sensible precaution when a political opponent asked for a private interview. Tim repeated what he had told his own leader, and I remember how, as we shut the front gate behind us as we left, he said, 'You know, the old captain's not a bad sort of fellow, after all.'

Do these things matter? They helped to make a man who, with his wife's full support, stood four-square for what was right on every issue, public or private, in the borough council, and as a shop steward in the steel construction works. This continued throughout the war, when he worked on the secret construction of the artificial port, code-named 'Mulberry', for the invasion of Europe. It continued again when the Rignalls went to America for some years and met many key trade union leaders. It continued till Tim, back in England, could only do light work. He took a job as a messenger in a shipbuilding yard, and made it a means to build friendships throughout the company, including the chairman of the board of directors. (I heard the chairman describe him as 'my best friend'.) His steadfast service won him the honour of a gold medal from his trade union, the Boilermakers' Society.

For every clear-cut experience like these two there are many experiences less conclusive, vague, frustrating sometimes, and difficult to assess. Sometimes there were rebuffs; often an initiative failed to produce the desired results. Quite often the whole concept of moral re-armament was attacked by certain people, its principles misrepresented, and those associated with it accused of all sorts of misdemeanours. Now and then, I came in for some of such criticisms myself. This was, however, to be expected. It was not so hard to cope with as internal conflicts, the times when I felt that nothing was worth while, that everything I touched went wrong, that I would never reach even a reasonable standard of behaviour, let alone succeed in my undertakings. Usually, however, a way out from such a state could be found fairly quickly. Action was most commonly the solution, to do something positive to help someone else. That was the best cure for introspection and depression.

In business too, of course, set-backs were not uncommon. A determined effort to reach an agreement on some issue would be met with hostility. Promises of new business would be broken. Some move of mine, perhaps an attempt to conciliate someone, would be brushed off rudely, or an attempt at gentle tactics exploited as a weakness. I have even sat in a court of law and heard myself accused of conspiracy to put a man out of business. The action failed, but it was not a pleasant experience.

Suppose, however, these things had not happened. Suppose every project succeeded, every relationship developed smoothly and happily, and life had been free of set-backs, sourness, pain or boredom. How flavourless it would have been without disappointment, frustration, embarrassment or shame! Perhaps it has been for me, taken altogether, the best of all possible worlds.

16

Some Reassessments

I have indicated how successive factors have influenced my life, like floods laying down levels of alluvial soil. Some of these factors were not noticed at the time, or quite wrongly assessed, and it was only as I wrote this account that I began to see them differently. It may be of value to look again at these sources, and see what effects have flowed from them.

In some cases, they did their work, and a living contact with them ceased, or nearly so. I am hardly likely to go back to the Boy Scout movement now, though I retain a warm gratitude for my few years with them. My links with Christ's Hospital, in later life, though cordial, have not involved me deeply. There are many better qualified or better placed to help that unique school to carry on its work. I never exactly gave up cycling. Progressively, it was replaced by other activities.

An area in which much change did take place was in my attitude to organised religion. My blind hostility to it vanished fairly quickly when I found that certain of my first friends connected with Moral Re-Armament were in fact clergy, and were sensitive, helpful, normal people. More gradually, I began to see that some kind of framework, some structure made up of people, was essential if we were ever to have the new society I was trying to envisage and work for. In this light, the traditional churches had a different appearance.

My criticisms of them did not disappear. In fact, nowadays, after a long membership and participation in the church – it always seems to me more 'the church' than individual or sectional churches – I am probably more critical than ever. There is a difference, though, between standing outside and saying, 'they are wrong', and being a part of something with the right and the obligation to say, 'We still need much change.'

After we moved back to live in Central London in 1958, we decided to shift our allegiance from the Congregational Church to the Church of England. One reason was that our parish church was nearer and livelier, and I felt quite at home with their services after six years at a school with a strong Anglican tradition. The more important one was that the old reasons which divided the church into separate fragments hundreds of years ago seem to be to a large extent irrelevant today. In those days it seemed to matter enormously how the church was governed or organised, what forms of worship were preferred, or what meaning people put on some particular paragraph in the church's sacred writings. In an age when vast numbers of people profess no religion, or run their lives as if religion has no relation to daily life, the details of belief or practices seem unimportant compared with mankind's basic and terrible need for some principles to live by.

Moreover, those who now profess no faith (and are maybe generations away from exposure to people who both professed a faith and allowed it to govern their lives) rarely respond to the formulae and practices of a century ago. Just as in the materialistic communist world the church is officially treated as being mainly a historical curiosity, no longer relevant, so in the largely materialist 'free' world religion is treated by many as having no importance to what are regarded as real issues, like earning a living, national defence, or politics.

In fact, my change of attitude is more than the change from an outsider's viewpoint to that of an insider. It comes from the fact that I am constantly asking myself, 'What is God's plan for the world?' as well as the corollary question of how the answer applies to me. I don't intend to answer that question here, if only because I get a different answer every time I ask it. It is much more interesting for every person to seek his or her individual answer. But in doing so it helps to consider what functions organised religion should have in the ideal plan, and how we can move forward towards them.

I have explained how much I owe to my parents, often for things I did not adequately value at the time. The same could be said of my family generally. I certainly needed a changed attitude there. Just after we were married, Constance suggested we should invite visits from certain relations. I am ashamed to say that I brutally remarked: 'I married you, not the whole of your family.' This attitude, for far too long, barred me off from much contact with her and my families. And how much I missed through that. Since this has been put right, we have discovered and shared in rich treasures of human nature, which have delighted and challenged us.

One of the cousins I at first selfishly shunned was, like her husband, qualified as a chartered accountant. Not long after he completed his studies with outstanding success, he developed a strong conviction that he was in the wrong profession, and should have been a doctor. To make this possible, the two of them agreed that they should live on her earnings as a professional accountant alone during his six years of medical school. This strenuous apprenticeship developed into a long and fruitful marriage. Another cousin, widowed, crippled and at an age where most people are thinking merely of survival, was touched by the difficulties of immigrants to the country in learning the language, and finding a place in their new society. She offered to teach English, best done in these circumstances on the basis of one teacher, one student. Though she was house-bound by her disability, the authorities responded to her enthusiasm, first sending teachers to train her to teach, and then the students for her to help.

I have also had the deep pleasure of exploring the ramifications of our two families in several countries. The thirty-odd cousins in Australia, of three generations, include some rich personalities. Three of the girls have married 'new Australians', of Greek, Italian, and Polish descent — but all of them extremely Australian! But probably the most dramatic example there, to the eyes of a city man like me, is that of the father and son who with one helper cultivate some ten square miles of wheatland. They raise sheep, too, but say that the main purpose of that is to keep down the weeds between harvest-time and the new sowing.

The even wider ramifications are most marked in the Irish Republic, where there is a wide scattering of Ledwiths, Ledwiches, Ledwidges, and Ledwicks, who are all reputed to descend from an original incursion from England in AD 1200. I find it strangely moving to be linked by blood so closely to a country which has known centuries of trouble, but which also sent saints and scholars out to many parts of the world. One of the more romantic members of the clan was Frank Ledwidge of Slane in County Meath. Son of a village schoolmaster, he worked as a farm labourer and on the roads, though it is said that his mother once took him to the Hill of Tara, where the High Kings of Ireland held council, and as she swept her arm around, said, 'All these were once Ledwidge lands.' He studied, and became well known as a poet, and part of the Irish renaissance. His verses appear in many Irish and English anthologies. They remind me a little of the English nature poet John Clare, but Ledwidge, a Gaelic speaker, carried over into his poems the old Gaelic rhyming schemes, with internal rhymes and alliteration. He was also a pioneer trade unionist, and an organiser of the strongly nationalist Irish Volunteers. When war came in 1914, he joined the British Army because, he said, if the Germans beat the British, Ireland would never get independence. In 1917, at the age of thirty, he was killed in France. But what a gloriously Irish life!

In recent years, we are fortunate to have had four major family reunions, of forty or so relations, three when Australian cousins visited England, and one for a golden wedding. Ages varied from a few months to eighty-odd years, and it was remarkable to find how cheerfully and fruitfully the generations mingled. In Britain and other 'developed' societies, the family seems to have been devalued in this century. Old people are increasingly isolated in special accommodation. Society is more layered into different generations. We need to rediscover the varied joys of the extended family, which is still cherished in Asia, Africa, and the Latin America. It involves responsibilities, too, but they may prove to be a fair price for the benefits they bring when we all learn to care more for each other.

Those last words may be a clue to what is the basic ingredient of my life as it has grown to be – not that I am complacent about it. I feel that it is still only a shadow of what life could be, to a person sufficiently wholehearted. From the very first contact in 1933 with those people who were later labelled collectively 'Moral Re-Armament', I experienced a vast amount of teaching and training. It was almost all informal, and much of it was transmitted by the force of example. In those first years, we often saw Frank Buchman, the 'founding father' of the work, who was much in England. He was constantly training people, with anecdotes, mnemonics, and advice. Often, too, it was by example, as when I was one of some dozens who were deep in consultation about some major moves, in a sitting-room at Brown's Hotel, London; the door opened a foot, and one of the young Oxford graduates recently recruited put his head into the room. He was about to duck out again, seeing our absorption, when Dr Buchman caught sight of him. At once, he broke into the discussion, saying, 'Edward! You're off to Scandinavia, aren't you? Have you got enough money?' The head came forward again, with reassurances and goodbyes, the door shut, and we resumed our conferring.

The picture, however, has remained with me for half a century. What it says to me still is simple: nothing is more important than people and their needs, all their needs, and at any moment. One of Buchman's common sayings was, 'You must treat every person as a royal soul.' Try that on for size!

In 1945, just after the war ended, every ship available was crowded with troops (and a few civilians) returning from Europe to the USA and Canada. One of the deprivations of the war years had been the lack of the normal contacts between countries, and this had of course affected that loose association of people who were dedicated to the programme of moral re-armament. It was therefore a joy to hear that our transatlantic bonds could be revived, when two of our friends (senior men from industry) were accepted for passage to America on the *Queen Mary*. They were quite happy to sleep four to a single cabin, and queue in shifts for simple meals with (if I remember rightly) eighteen thousand US troops. And a dozen or so met with them for a farewell meal at Brown's Hotel.

Food was still short. On the way to this function, I saw the rare sight of tomatoes for sale from a barrow. It would be a real treat for my family. Thus, when I arrived at Brown's I offered the porter in charge of the cloakroom not only my bowler hat, coat and umbrella to care for whilst I was in the private dining-room, but a paper bag of rather overripe tomatoes. He accepted them with dignity and kindness, but as I was turning away, he asked: 'Excuse me, sir, but are you by any chance connected with the Oxford Group?' I said, 'Well, yes, I suppose I am.' He went on, 'I thought I recognised some of the gentlemen who went upstairs before you. I just wanted to mention, if you will allow me, that the very first time Doctor Buchman came to this hotel, I carried his bags up to his room.' I went away, marvelling. What was it that made the porter regard this routine service as a treasured memory? What had been said or done? Could it be that my everyday contacts with ordinary people ought to be of such quality that they would produce similar reactions?

At least, I felt I should try to be alert to people's needs and potentialities, and seek to meet those needs whenever and however they became apparent. Once in those early days I was being driven through South London by one of my new friends, Arthur Strong, a professional photographer of note. I was telling him of a talk I had had with the minister of our Congregational Church. In excitement, he burst out, 'But don't you understand what he was saying to you? He is longing to experience change in his own life. He was appealing to you for help. You must see him and give him the chance to talk further.' He pulled up at the next telephone box. Somewhat dazed, I got out. I telephoned the minister. We did meet, but nothing dramatic happened. Still, it almost certainly helped in my building a positive and helpful relationship with him. This was needed, for in the past he had found me a difficult customer. Later, he asked Constance and me to help him in preparing candidates for church membership. For someone who had been as anti-church as I, this was a novel experience.

In a hundred ways my wife and I gave priority to whatever seemed to be a part of the programme of changing the world by change in people. The pattern of our lives changed a great deal, becoming much more flexible and inclined to suffer lightning amendments. Of course, my working life had to follow a framework. I had contracted to do a certain job, and it was important that I did it conscientiously. Outside working hours, we were ready to go anywhere and do anything which seemed likely to forward the plan.

This led to touches with all kinds of people, in Parliament, the church, trade unions, newspaper editors (one in particular became a good friend), and many circles of activity with which I otherwise had no touch. Moreover, the touches themselves were often a little bizarre, since if one seeks to help with all a person needs, in every field, one may be doing something very dull and obscure on minute, and follow it by something quite extravagant. This reminds me that at my first big conference, in Oxford, of what we then called the Oxford Group, one of the main meetings was presided over by a rather elegant undergraduate, son of a Bristol family of shipowners. And I happened to see him before the next meeting, setting out chairs.

It is still the case that I rarely know all about what is to happen the next day, or the next week. We habitually keep our programme as flexible as we can, in order to adapt to the individual needs of people. Not long ago, we lent our flat for a tea-party given by Penelope Thwaites, the Australian concert pianist, for various of her friends in the world of music after one of her recitals at Wigmore Hall. (The occasion was somewhat different from past cycling activities, as it also was from the years of deskwork and legwork in insurance.) When all the guests had gone, I said to Penny, 'I suppose that now you'll be glad to get home for a rest.' 'Good heavens, no,' she replied, 'I'm far too tense and excited for that.' My wife looked at me, and more or less simultaneously we realised that Penny had probably had nothing much to eat, in looking after the crowd of guests. So we suggested something to eat. This was warmly welcomed. A huge fresh pot of tea was made, and all the food we could find was spread over the table. And she talked almost non-stop for three solid hours. No great truths emerged; no deep spiritual issues were discussed; her need at that point was food, tea, and a chance to reduce the pressures to normal.

One of my godsons asked if I would lend him a moderately

substantial sum of money to complete a project he was engaged in. He would pay me back out of the profits after some months. I told him that I was averse to lending money to friends. On at least one occasion when I had done so, I had lost both the money and the friendship. Then I gave his request very serious thought. As a result, I told him that I would not lend to him but, feeling my responsibility as his godfather, make a gift to him of the sum involved. He protested, saying that he only wanted a loan. I insisted, and we ended by agreeing that I would regard it as a gift. If he wanted to repay it later, that was up to him, but I would not give it another thought. It therefore came as a pleasant surprise that after the project was completed, he repaid the money.

These incidents are not important of themselves. They merely illustrate the principle that one has to think how each issue shall be approached if the real needs of the person concerned are to be met. I deeply believe that every individual can change, and move on to the right road for life (or return to it), but it is impossible to tell what will prompt a person to respond in the right way. All one can hope to do is to provide opportunities in which the right choices can be made – whatever they may be.

What should be our aims? What kind of human future should we work for, and what kind of person? One of my visits to Northern Ireland occurred when I was asked to go and help co-ordinate arrangements for a party from North America, some thirty strong, who wanted to see for themselves what was happening. They were on their way home from an international conference for Moral Re-Armament in Switzerland. The party included black and white from the United States, and English- and French-speaking Canadians. It was a bad time. Twenty-two bombs exploded in Belfast on the day they arrived. However, they were well looked after, saw some grim sights, and met a wide cross-section of the people. At one point, a private meeting was arranged with about a hundred Irish, ranging from Unionist politicians to some of the Catholic housewives who later helped to develop the 'peace movement'.

The North Americans, with a touch of genius, appointed as their main spokesman a chief of the Indians from the Canadian prairies. I happened to see a good deal of him in those few days. A big, taciturn man, he brightened up visibly whenever he came within visual contact of horses or cattle grazing up on the vividly green Irish fields. For the meeting, he proudly wore a great feathered head-dress and decorated buckskins, and he read out a message of sympathy from the Queen's

Lieutenant-Governor in Alberta. His own speech was plain and short, and held the Irish in a fascinated silence. I can still remember the gist of it. Approximately, it was like this: 'We have come from America to learn from you what is happening here, and to ask you if there is anything at all we can do to help. I am a simple man. I used to be a drunkard and a waster. Thanks to Moral Re-Armament, I am finished with that, and so my people elected me as their chief. Because I wanted my people to know that I am a simple man, I refused the government allowance which they give to our chiefs, and I support my family by what I earn by driving a school bus. Please tell us what difficulties you have here, and if we can help.'

I feel small before a man like that. It makes me wonder yet again what should be our aims. Most of all, we need one great central aim, to which everything else can be related, and by which it can be tested.

Frank Buchman often told the story of his first experiments in clothing with action his convictions about world change through change in individuals, when he held a post at Pennsylvania State College early in this century. Although hundreds of people were involved in the experiments, which also reached out to Harvard and other universities, his strategy was focused on three individuals, the dean of the college, the ruffianly character who illicitly supplied the students with huge quantities of booze, and a cultivated and popular student from Virginia named Blair Buck. To all these, Buchman gave detailed attention, and each helped in the developments which have of course been recorded elsewhere. It is enough to say here that many individuals experienced drastic and permanent change in their lives, the college revived from a moribund condition, and a number of wider issues were affected.

When the time came for Buck to leave college, Buchman asked him what he proposed to do. I feel fairly certain that the hope was that he would join Buchman as an associate in his distinctive work. Buck, however, said that he felt he had to do something about education for the black Americans. It was very interesting to me, therefore, to hear Blair Buck say at a conference fifty years later that he was still working on education for black Americans.

It is fairly well known that the big international movement called Alcoholics Anonymous was what would be called, if it were a matter of science or technology, a 'spin-off' of Moral Re-Armament. Two men, one of them a doctor, affected by Buchman's work, adapted some of the principles they had learned in order to attack a problem which they felt, rightly, was one of great importance and danger.

In a different sphere, Buchman and his colleagues affected those developments from which emerged the European Economic Community. It was not that they promoted this or any other political proposal. Rather, it was in helping to bridge the gaps which existed between individuals and countries in Western Europe. War between French and Germans had gone on more or less constantly for many decades until the Battle of Waterloo in 1815. Half a century later, in 1870, there was another major war. Forty years later in 1914 there came another, and after only a twenty years' gap a third. What gap would there be from 1945 before fighting began again? A few politicians saw the danger, especially Robert Schuman, Foreign Minister of France, a man brought up in Lorraine under German rule, and Konrad Adenauer, Chancellor of the German Federal Republic. Their aims on this issue were similar, yet their co-operation was not easy, and neither wholly trusted the other. The first step was the plan drawn up by Jean Monnet of France for the uniting of the French and German coal and steel industries. If this was carried through, how could the two countries ever fight each other? Two months after the agreement was signed in 1957, Adenauer wrote in a letter to Buchman, 'Moral Re-Armament has played an invisible but effective part in bridging differences of opinion between negotiating parties, and has kept before them the object of peaceful agreement in the search for the common good which is the true purpose of human life.'

There have been developments elsewhere which bear a certain similarity to this French-German situation. One was the ending of the civil war in Rhodesia, now renamed Zimbabwe. Another was the astonishing surge of growth in war-ruined Japan. In these situations, too, Moral Re-Armament was significantly involved, though it did not specifically promote the moves which developed, and other forces also contributed to produce the results. What does seem to be the case is that if a sufficient group of people in a situation actively promote the acceptance of absolute moral standards and an inspired course of action, unexpected and widespread change may result. Why and how it happens sometimes seems a mystery.

Things like these often come back to me, as I try to assess the years past, and take stock of my position as I enter the closing stages of life. What part I have had in great events has been marginal – a brush here, a word there. Most of my days do not appear to have had more significance than those of the average of mankind. One must, however, do what one can. And in this old body there is still a trace of the fifteen-year-old boy who sat in the library of Christ's Hospital with his head bent over Tennyson's 'Ulysses'. The tramping rhythm clanged in his head like brazen bells:

> 'Much have I seen and known; cities of men
> And manners, climates, councils, governments ...
> I am a part of all that I have met;
> Yet all experience is an arch wherethrough
> Gleams that untravelled world, whose margin fades
> For ever and for ever when I move ...
> Old age hath yet his honour and his toil ...
> Some work of noble note may yet be done ...
> 'Tis not too late to seek a newer world ...'

I knew the whole poem by heart once.

17

The Rewards of Age

More emphasis is placed, as a rule, on the disabilities which age brings than on the rewards of age. It is easier for me than for some others to redress this balance, since for me the weaknesses and handicaps of age have crept on me rather slowly. From the age of fifteen, when I had a month in the school infirmary, I was never an in-patient in a hospital until I was over seventy. Even then, my brief periods in hospital were for operations which restored my hearing to a very good level, and my eyesight to quite a good standard, too. When I developed back pains, associated with a spinal curvature and arthritis, I asked my doctor why they should suddenly afflict me now. He replied, 'That's the wrong question. You should ask, how did your body manage to cope with your condition without pain until you were well into the sixties?' And now treatment keeps it in check. So I am a fortunate person.

Mentally, too, I am not conscious of much deterioration. I should, therefore, be able to appreciate fully the advantages that come with the years.

In Asian countries I have visited, respect is paid to older people much more generally and obviously than in Europe and North America. When my wife and I were proposing to attend a conference in Japan, a candid friend said, 'If I may say so without offence, your age will be your primary asset.' And so it proved. It meant that additional weight was given to anything we said and did. This was quite refreshing, coming as we did from a culture where so much attention is focused on the young.

Why is it that grey hairs are so honoured in those countries? Mere survival is not a good enough reason. Is it perhaps experience that is being recognised? At the time I write, I am still associated with a certain international committee. I play a reduced part in its work, but several times I have been urged (and I think sincerely) to keep up my connection as long as possible. It is certainly not because I am the most intelligent of the group. But I am the oldest by a fair margin, and the only one who can look back to certain distant times, and say how problems were tackled then and what decisions were made. The same is the case in my connections with other organisations. And when I was training people for management, I found that the students never seemed to tire of hearing examples from the past, and especially of the mistakes I had made when I was in the early stages. And they never seemed to repeat my mistakes, though they managed to invent some quite original mistakes of their own.

Experience must, I think, be one of the treasures which is only available fully to those with a long life behind them. One does need, however, to recognise the value of what one has been through, to apply the lessons learned, and to be willing to share then with others, even if one may look a fool or a rogue as a result. I cannot remember ever actually losing face by admitting past faults – except in my own eyes. Perhaps it is that people identify more easily with someone who is not perfect. Or perhaps they already know or suspect the failings we are tempted to hide.

For me in particular it has taken many years to accept one rather fundamental fact, that character is developed in two ways, almost in two different dimensions. One is action, the other contemplation. For most of my life, attention has been focused on doing things. The other angle, that of being or becoming something, has been very much neglected.

Take, for example, a task like writing this book. My inclination is to keep hammering at it, making notes, writing and re-writing, even when I do not see clearly how it is developing, and where the thoughts in it are pointing. But the sounder approach, when I am at a loss, or even hesitant, is to put it aside, perhaps to do something else, until a line of thought has developed, seeping out of my mind like moisture into a hole dug in a dry riverbed. It is even more important to develop this kind of thinking where it is not attached to a certain task. We need times when we open our minds to new concepts, to the reassessment of fixed ideas, to the ripening or solidifying of those vague beginnings which may disappear if no chance is given for them to be fully considered. Bernard Eyre-Walker, a landscape painter who was a good friend of our family, had a method of working which illustrates this principle. He would take a small tent up into the mountains, find a promising site, and spend two or three days just strolling about and looking. Then he would get out his water-colours, and produce several pictures, working flat out. Incidentally, Bernard overcame what seemed to me to be a unique handicap in a painter. He was colour blind. His wife usually went with him, and told him which colours to use, and they were carefully kept in the same order in his box. I suppose, in a way, it was a parallel to Beethoven's handicap of deafness.

I have even discovered, in quite recent years, the joy of doing absolutely nothing occasionally. But I daren't indulge in that too often.

At times, I get down to serious study of some important work which is worth reading from cover to cover. This is rarely pleasure for me; my mind turns naturally more to the trivial and ephemeral, but I have read with care all three volumes of Solzhenitsyn's *Gulag Archipelago*, Gibbon's *Decline and Fall of the Roman Empire*, the Bible three times right through (as well as countless dippings), and so on. These activities are less for the pursuit of knowledge than for mental exercise and (dare I say?) character training.

But the most valuable part of my belated attempt to upgrade the neglected side of my nature is in the morning times of quiet thought which I first began in 1933. I hunger for them now, and it is often an effort to break off for breakfast. Sometimes, it is true, nothing much seems to happen; what notes I make may be fairly routine thoughts, things to attend to, ruminations over what is happening in the world, even a record of my feelings and reactions. However, one never knows when something unusual will break in, a new light on some problem, an unexpected revelation of some kind. I grow always more certain that one's mind can develop contacts, however imperfect, with something greater out there, something richer, more positive, more satisfying.

To the other valuable things which accrue with age can be added the loss of some illusions. Illusions have their value. It is sometimes hard to draw a line between illusion and the dreams which over the centuries have inspired many of man's boldest voyages of exploration into the unknown. Columbus set out to sail to China, and thought he had arrived there when he landed on an American island. But this applies not only to the geographical unknown, but to all the possibilities that lie hidden in the future, from cures for diseases to hopes for a Utopian society.

Many illusions, however, we are better without. Some of mine have had quite a battering, even where they have not been utterly destroyed.

One is the illusion that I am right. My wife would tell you that I still suffer from it far too often. Yet I often do question its validity. I often do, in considering an issue, weigh the assumption that I am right against the alternative that I am wrong. I suppose it might be wiser to start from the point that I am probably wrong, and see if a better and different appreciation of the point displaces this first opinion. It is an illusion that is very widespread. I once heard a priest of the Church of England say that it could be useful for Christians to have contact with those of other faiths, 'but we must never forget that we are right, and they are wrong'. I was struck dumb, which was a pity, as that good man ought not to have been left at that point. If I say that my religious beliefs are right, and all others wrong, it implies that I understand God. What could be more wrong than that? It may be proper to say that I believe certain things to be right. That is another thing entirely. I also believe that the earth goes round the sun. There is much evidence to support that belief, too, but if I say it does go round the sun, can I be sure I am right?

Another illusion which I have surrendered with some reluctance is the illusion that I know. In actual fact, I usually do not know, and when I have some knowledge it is often inaccurate or incomplete. Even with the more serious general knowledge quiz programmes which infest radio and television (and which fascinate me horribly) I tend to score between twenty-five and fifty per cent, and in some areas of knowledge, like music, I am almost wholly ignorant. Here again it would be much safer if I always, instead of sometimes, started from the assumption that I do not know.

Other illusions deal with more limited fields. One is that some person or group is irreconcilably an enemy towards me and towards those who think as I do, or is irrecoverably lost in error or in evil. In point of fact, anyone can change. Even I have experienced change to some degree. And I think of a man like Jim Crooks, who some years ago was a branch secretary of the National Union of Mineworkers in Northumberland. A committed Communist for many years, he was known for his total antagonism to anyone who in his eyes stood for capitalism, including of course the local management of the National Coal Board. As a result, production at the Linton colliery where he worked had fallen to such a level that the pit faced closure, with the loss of over a thousand jobs. Then Jim began to change. The effect of this (as newspaper files will support) was the saving of those jobs, and a lasting difference in his whole approach to life. At an early stage in this change a small group waiting for a plane at Geneva airport included Jim, myself and our respective wives. We had all been at a conference for Moral Re-Armament. Jim suggested coffee. I had no Swiss currency, so he paid. As we sat drinking it, he suddenly began to laugh, and went on laughing. 'Fancy me,' he spluttered, 'me of all people, buying coffee for a capitalist.' I graciously accepted the appellation, forbearing from telling him that at that time I had absolutely no capital of my own, and did not even own our home or car. It would have spoiled his pleasure. I think it was the next day that Jim saw the pit manager and offered to work together with him to save the pit. Which they did.

Then there is the dangerous illusion that confrontation is inevitable between the Communist and non-Communist worlds. I used to accept this as being so, but I rejected it long ago, mainly on the basis of my impressions of the Communists I have met, Russian, Yugoslav and others. But the alternative is not the appeasement which some advocate. The alternative is a real change towards a just society in both sections of the world.

I have also learnt to reject the assumption that economic considerations control events. They do affect events, but it is people who control them. If it appears that economic considerations are leading towards a disaster, all that is needed to change the situation is for one or more people (perhaps many people) to say 'no', and to follow this by action. An example in 1985 of a change in economic trends was when most of the leading 'pop' musicians in Britain and the United States joined together to raise scores of millions of pounds for famine relief in Africa. I suppose that the salient features of the pop music scene have always been an extreme individualism, and the making of large profits by some individuals. Suddenly, they worked together as a group in a regular campaign of unselfishness, and this substantially affected world events.

There was an earlier example of feeding the hungry, involving some five thousand people, who only had available five loaves and two small fish. Many believe that this was made possible by divine intervention overruling natural laws, and multiplying the material available. I have sometimes wondered if it was not something else, the initial decision to share this small supply of food prompting many other people present to produce a package here and a package there which had been put aside for future needs, and to add it to the common store. If so, such a widespread change in human nature could have been just as miraculous as the physical miracle which is more usually thought to have taken place.

On economic issues generally, I tend to balk at solemn references to 'the economic system'. Quite seriously, I do not think there is an economic system. It would be more honest to say that in some areas a degree of order has been attempted in a general condition of economic chaos. The British government recently published one of its regular batches of statistics about money matters. One group of figures bore a note that they were all subject to a margin of error of twenty per cent. Twenty per cent! Are they sure it should not have been twenty-one per cent? Or fifty per cent? Economics should be classed with the social sciences and psychology as 'not an exact science'. It is not really a science at all. It is quite rare for two economists to agree on anything.

I suppose that at one time there was some degree of certainty about economic matters. The difficulties of travel and distrust of neighbouring tribes meant that only a small area could be considered by any one 'economist'. The goods available were there to be seen and counted, and if there was any kind of currency then, there were only a finite number of cowrie shells or elephant tusks to count. Today it is different. The great bulk of transactions are based on credits and debits which are just paper entries. Increasingly, they are not even that. They are electrical impulses stored in computers.

However, economics is a useful tool, even if it is not an exact science. We would be in a far worse fix if there was no attempt to measure resources and to assess the consequences of different financial, trade and tax policies. It is far better to have an imperfect picture of these things than none at all.

But the biggest weakness about economics and the statistics which are thrown at us and argued over by the politicians, is that they rarely acknowledge or allow for the human factor. A wave of feeling amongst ordinary people can upset all their calculations. Anyone who doubts that statement can get it confirmed by a two-minute chat with any stockbroker. For example, a great company can declare an enormous profit, but if that profit is slightly smaller than people on the stock exchange expect, the price of the company's shares will go down, not up. And an unfounded rumour can wipe billions of pounds off the value of shares (the quoted value, at least) in an hour.

Economic circumstances, therefore, are to a large extent subordinate to human impulses. If the leaders of mankind, or those they lead, wish to get our material affairs in order, they need first to study how to foster right motives in people, and thus right actions. Is there an alternative to the chaos which reflects the conflicts of different people's selfishness? I am sure there is. It may be much simpler than we think. It may just be a dedication to what is right. That is simple, but it is not easy. It would imply that every issue must be considered on its merits, and that a valid proposal from a stranger or an opponent would be welcomed just as much as if it were our own, or from 'our side'.

I might add one more illusion which I have been glad to shed. A respected friend remarked long ago that he had always assumed that those in high positions who directed (or appeared to direct) our destinies were people of a different kind, more moral, wide of vision, public-spirited by nature, extraordinarily intelligent and wise. As the years went by, he said, he had penetrated more and more into these circles, until he met some who might be considered to be at the very top. But he never met any of the super-beings he had expected. To a certain extent, I have had a similar experience, and I agree with my friend. Taken by and large, these people are just like you and me.

At dinner on a certain occasion, I found myself placed next to an imposing African lady. She was, I was told, the sister of Jomo Kenyatta, then President of Kenya. Whatever does one talk about to such a person, I asked myself in momentary panic. Kenya had just emerged into independence, after the horrible experience of the semi-nationalist, semi-mystical Mau Mau murders and civil war. Kenyatta, not long before a prisoner in jail, was in some people's minds a vicious criminal, in other people's minds the saviour of his great country.

I myself had never been in Africa, and was deeply ignorant of African ways and African needs. I cast round in my mind for a way out, and by elementary reasoning selected a topic. Hesitantly, I asked what the crops were like in Kenya that year. Her face lit up. She started to expound with enthusiasm, and I had nothing to do but listen. And how foolish I had been to be in some awe of this warm-hearted lady.

There is something more which has grown in me with the passage of years. It has come into focus only as I have compiled this account, though inklings have been present for some time. This is that life, existence, the cosmos, however you prefer to regard it, develops in accordance with certain natural laws. And they are inevitable laws. They do not change, however inconvenient we find them. Some of them deal with physical facts, the properties of matter, the law of gravity, the movements of the stars and planets, and such. Others are more difficult to define, but are no less real, and they deal with causes and their effects.

I had hoped to define these laws, but I find that I can not. They are too great for me. They are associated with those absolute moral standards to which I have referred. But the gist of the great laws is that if we do what is right, we build on rock. Our inner integrity holds. Whether we succeed or fail becomes irrelevant. The issue is not that. The issue is whether we have done right.

If however we turn from what is right, we head straight into trouble, and possibly into destruction. The least we can expect is complications, uncertainty, a scrabbling for a makeshift remedy for what we have done.

In recent decades there have, I think, been many glaring examples of the deliberate pursuit of ignoble aims. The obsession with 'economic' objectives is one. It is another way of describing the pursuit of material wealth as an aim in itself, the continual acquisition of more and more things, or their equivalent. From owning one motor-car per family, it is considered natural to move on to two, then no doubt three, four, five. Houses are considered more desirable homes according to how thickly they are cluttered with rarely-used electrical appliances, special knives and special dishes for exotic foods, books that are unread, tapes and records that are not listened to. No wonder some parts of the world get poorer if for some of us it is considered vital to keep getting richer and richer. A journalist once asked me if I could explain why my country's gross national product had been increasing more slowly, percentage-wise, than was the case in certain other countries. I said the first thing which came into my mind, which was, 'Why do you assume that it is a good thing that a country's gross national product should increase? If by decreasing ours by ten per cent we could guarantee better conditions in the poorest countries, would not that be an advance?' He closed his notebook.

There is much satisfaction to be gained from deliberately seeking a simpler life-style, and from shunning luxuries. My wife and I do without a car now. Occasionally, it is inconvenient, but it saves us a lot of hassle. On balance, it is a gain. My sister, on the subject of Christmas presents, remarked, 'I think we have got to the point where we would rather have less possessions than accumulate more.'

Instant pleasure is another false aim which is held out as desirable. This is the cult which underlies many of the social ills which are being more and more openly deplored, such as the selfish use of sex, which is often associated with its twin of indiscriminate violence, and the abuse of drugs (which we are now beginning to admit includes alcohol and tobacco). 'I want it, so I must have it, and have it now.' It is an attitude which cannot fail to make impossible any kind of society attractive to all who share in it. I think it was in 1971 that a friend in the United States sent me a book called *The Greening of America*. It urged everyone without exception to develop a new life-style, which would transform the experience of the individual, and bring in a sort of heaven on earth. The recommended experiences were to wear blue jeans, to make regular use of drugs, especially marihuana, and so 'expand one's consciousness' in hallucinations, to soak oneself in psychedelic music, to let one's personal aggressive feelings have full play, to throw off all restraints on sexual activity, and generally 'to do one's own thing'. I remember querying what happened when two people's 'own things' happened to be directly contrary to each other. And what if one had a sudden urge to sit down in the middle of a motorway? But it was a more serious matter than that. It was a deliberate call for self-indulgence as a settled policy. Similar calls have come from many other sources, including some psychologists and some theorists in the field of 'social sciences'.

What are the aims we humans should pursue? When my son was about to leave school, he had no clear idea what career he should choose. I saw his headmaster, who strongly urged that he should aim at the top grades of the Civil Service 'because that is where the power is going to be in the years to come'. Even if he had been right in this judgement, it seemed to me utterly wrong for anyone to dedicate his life to achieving power. I am glad to say the head's views were not accepted, and that after some experiments, and even what some might consider one or two false starts, my son did develop a career which seems suited to him, and from which he gets considerable satisfaction.

However, it is plain enough that many of us, much of the time, have the wrong aims. No wonder that the results are bad. Those results are displayed in the headlines of every newspaper ever day.

Fortunately, there is a rider to this inevitable sequence of cause and effect, to the law which cannot be broken, the rule that if we do wrong, we will suffer for it. For some reason, we are quite often relieved of the full consequences of our follies and wrongdoing. Justice is tempered with mercy. We are allowed, sometimes, to put right what was wrong, and to start afresh. We, who were once told to forgive those who wrong us, not once or twice but seventy times seven times, need ourselves to be forgiven more often than that. If we were not forgiven, I suppose, the things we try to slur over as 'human failings' would wreck the whole show, and any kind of concerted progress would be impossible.

The older I grow, the more certain I am that all things are subject to law. But there is also forgiveness. Which is just as well. Each of us tends to be like a small child in a high chair, spilling its food, often by clumsiness, sometimes by wilful naughtiness. And always forgiven.

We do make things hard for ourselves. I once heard the matron of a large London hospital speak at a big public meeting on the subject of national health. Her theme was that the health services, and in particular the hospitals, could easily cope with all that was needed for the care and cure of the sick, injured and disabled with the funds immediately available, subject to one condition. This condition was the elimination of unnecessary cases, which occupied beds needed for legitimate patients. She listed the cases she considered to be unnecessary. It began with road accidents caused by drink, carelessness, or aggression. Stomach ulcers and heart troubles caused by the worry of moneymaking were a big group, also chest and other diseases due to excessive smoking, and unwanted pregnancies (even, she commented in an aside, among her own nurses). There were other classes which anyone can think of, and add. Is a clearer example needed of the fact that if we do not keep to the rules, we head into trouble?

Perhaps, then, the greatest treasure the years have piled up for me is the growing certainty that there is sense in the scheme of things, that by following the rules we can avoid most ills, and that even when we fail, we can begin afresh.

18

Completion

Some time ago there was a very unusual programme shown on British television. It was a documentary, dealing with an enclosed order of nuns. Ordinarily, there would have been no possibility at all of the convent being opened to public scrutiny, since the central principle of it was that its members should be shut off from the world. However, it was thought so important that outside people should understand the purpose of the institution that a temporary but drastic departure from the rules was decided upon, and the cameras and sound recording equipment were welcomed in, and allowed to go everywhere.

It was a good programme, thoughtful, unsensational, and deeply interesting. The sisters seemed to spend their entire time and energy in a strenuous programme of prayer and worship, plus the necessary housekeeping activities. One image stands out clearly in my mind, when a young nun was asked by the interviewer, 'But what is it that you actually do?' She was a very lovely girl, very intelligent, with an open guileless face, and she replied with a dazzling smile of pure rapture, 'Why, we're getting ready to die!'

What better aim could anyone have? Each of us knows the moment will come when the last full stop ends the story of his life. Each must hope that when that comes, he will make a good end, and will feel that his time was well spent. In practice, however, things are different. Most of us try not to think of the end of our time here. We refuse to do so. We tell ourselves it will not happen to us – although we know it will. We resolutely set our minds on other things. A surprisingly large proportion of people never even make a will, as if such an act would itself encourage death to creep up on us.

In this century, in the society in which I move, death is the taboo subject, more than any other. Any mention of it causes embarrassment. We fear it. 'The last enemy to be destroyed shall be death.' So wrote Saint Paul. But is death truly an enemy? Is it not just the last incident in our life here, even the culmination of it?

Our revulsion against death leads us into strange situations. Some doctors interpret their Hippocratic oath as obliging them to keep people alive at all costs, even if they are only technically alive. One appreciates the difficulty of decisions on border-line cases, when completely unexpected recoveries can happen, but I hope I shall be allowed to go in peace and dignity when my time comes, without people desperately striving to give me a few more hours or days of life. Not long ago a woman friend declined into her last illness. Blind and helpless, she was well cared for. The day came when the surgeon told her husband that there was a choice which she was no longer capable of making for herself. The husband must therefore choose for her. She could be kept alive for some months more, but in pain and completely helpless. Or she could be allowed to drift painlessly into her last sleep within a few hours. It was a hard choice. The husband chose the quicker end for the woman he loved, and the surgeon said, 'Thank God!' to the decision.

Another good friend of mine for many years was Campbell Milligan, the Australian surgeon whose brass plate was up in London's Harley Street, among so many other plates, for forty or fifty years. In the First World War he saved many lives in France with what were then novel operating techniques, and which brought him into frequent conflict with his more conservative superiors. Later, he was one of the leaders in his particular branch of surgery. I first met him in 1938 when he offered me a lift to London from Eastbourne on a black and stormy winter night. His wife Josie drove their open Rolls Royce with its flapping hood and side-curtains. On a right-hand bend, we met a fast car ripping through the rain in the middle of the road. Josie took to the grass, bumping up the kerb and down again, without a pause in her conversation. When I commented, she said, 'Oh, I learnt to drive in the bush.' She had done a chauffeur's training course at the Rolls works, so that she could service the car herself. But for short journeys in town she always cycled, through the dense traffic of Central London.

The time came when Josie fell gravely ill. Told there was no hope, Campbell insisted on having her at home, so that he could nurse her himself. I went round to see them one afternoon. She could not speak, but her eyes showed that she knew me, and she pressed my hand. When I left the bedroom, Campbell insisted that I sit down while he made tea for me. He was a man with a simple and direct faith in guidance from God. As I nibbled a biscuit, he said between sips of tea something like this: 'I've asked to be told how long we have got, and I understand Josie has two or three weeks, and I have two or three years.' It was as natural to him as when he said, in the same tone of voice, 'Have another cup of tea.' And he was right about the time they had remaining.

A different angle on the same basic issue was experienced by another friend of many years' standing. As a young woman she was working in Nigeria, where she was involved in a bad road accident. A truck pulled out of a line of fast traffic, and caused a head-on collision. She had multiple injuries. On her arrival at hospital, doctors pronounced her condition to be hopeless. Later, she recovered consciousness, with a vivid recollection that whilst out of touch a clear message had been given her to the effect that 'You cannot leave yet. Your work here is not finished.' Against all medical judgements, she made a good recovery, to be capable of living a normal life. That was thirty years ago. She is still working. One of her passions is to build understanding between Britain and Latin America, where her family has had links for nearly two hundred years. She was one of the first Britons to revisit Argentina after the end of the fighting in the Falkland Islands.

How will I respond when my time to go arrives? Will I accept it without demur, without fear or fuss? I hope I will, though it is a lot to hope for. My record so far is not good. I flinch from pain, and rebel against any sickness which comes my way – initially, at any rate. And when someone close to me dies, my first reaction has always been remorse – if only I had not done this or that, if only I had been more caring, thoughtful, active in doing good to that person. One thing I am sure of is that I do not want knowledge of the approaching end to be held back from me. I may be frightened by it, but I do demand the chance to prepare. 'To make my peace with God' is the old phrase. First, however, I would have to make my peace with myself.

There may be no warning. None knows the time or the way in which it will come. And always there will be something one hoped to do tomorrow.

> 'Is life a boon?
> If so, it must befall
> That death whene'er he call
> Must call too soon.'

So wrote W.S. Gilbert in one of his more serious moments in *The Yeomen of the Guard.*

Yet it seems strange to me that we flinch so much from 'the last enemy', when the whole of nature shows how death is one of the facts of life. All kinds of life prey on other kinds all the time. How many tadpoles even achieve maturity? One in a thousand? How many cod's eggs? One in a million? Nature squanders life in vast quantities, content that a few individuals survive.

One could go further than that, and remind ourselves, on the widespread evidence of fossils, that species, too, die out when their time is up. Some people would have us see the extinction of any species, animal or vegetable, as a tragedy. Personally, I drop no tears for the departure of the sabre-tooth tiger, or even the dodo, and I have no urge (as some have) to go to great trouble and expense to preserve a few rare predator birds, without sympathy for the hundreds of songbirds and small mammals which each predator will kill and eat in its lifetime. This should not be read as an attack on all conservationists. I plead only for a sense of proportion and balance in these matters. Historically, we must expect that different species will disappear, whatever man does or neglects to do.

Meanwhile, we face a further mystery. What happens after death? Not long after my father died, I went to see my mother. I told her of some comic incident, at which she laughed heartily. 'How Dad would have enjoyed that!' she commented, and then said, after a moment's pause, 'I expect he is enjoying it. I have never doubted that there is life after death – though I think we have to go back to school, to learn the things we didn't learn here.' I rather think that is orthodox Christian doctrine, even if her mode of expression was somewhat informal.

Christians and many others believe there is life after death, even eternal life. The evidence for this, however, is not such as would stand up in a human court of law. An American collected a number of accounts by people who, through illness or injury, were pronounced dead by doctors, yet recovered. A fair number of them described experiences which had points in common with some of the others, such as being able to see their own apparently dead bodies from a point nearby. Some experienced bright lights, and meeting people they knew. Naturally, all the accounts were highly subjective, and incapable of corroboration. And they differed as often as they corresponded. So the general effect of the book, if reassuring, was unconvincing.

Since no one knows, it is natural that there are many views as to what form continued existence may take. Some think of a more remote or attenuated survival than of an actual rebirth of the individual, so that our existence continues through our descendants, or through people's memories of us, or through the influence of our life and work here, or even through the continuance of the human race of which we are a tiny part.

It is good that we do not know. It may help us to concentrate on what we should do and be in this life, to make it complete and to seek always to make it perfect. My deepest conviction is that there is a plan laid down for each of us, not only in outline, but in a wealth of detail, and with every contingency provided for. Even after each error or departure from the plan, there is a right way to follow, that very moment. And every experience, good or bad, can be used as a part of the whole plan.

Perhaps it is true, then, that each of us has the chance in his lifetime here to develop in a certain way, and to achieve certain things, and that every detail of that life can be used to help in that development and that achievement. If so, each can claim that his particular world has been for him the best of all possible worlds.

I would like to turn for the last word to one of England's best poets of this century. Edmund Blunden went from school (my old school, as it happens) almost at once into the savagery of the First World War. One of his poems of that period describes in a few touching lines how an army comrade in the blood-soaked Flanders trenches heard of the death in England of the girl he loved. The knowledge that he himself was unlikely to survive developed in his mind under this new pressure into certainty. The poem ends:

> 'And fortune cheats her end,
> And death draws nigh, a friend.'